NEW YORK

GERALD & MARC HOBERMAN

NEW YORK

GERALD & MARC HOBERMAN

PHOTOGRAPHS CELEBRATING THE CELEBRITY OF CITIES

TEXT BY RAY FURSE

THE GERALD & MARC HOBERMAN COLLECTION

CAPE TOWN • LONDON • NEW YORK

For Joanne and Laurence

STATUE OF LIBERTY

CONTENTS

Concept, design, photography, and production control
Gerald & Marc Hoberman
Cameras and lenses: **LEICA**
Camera: R8; Lenses: 19mm f2.8; 28mm f2.8; 50mm f1.4; 80mm f1.4; 100mm f2.8; 280mm f2.8; 800mm f6.3
Film: **KODAK**
Ektachrome 100 S Professional
Helicopter: **NEW YORK HELICOPTER CHARTER, INC.**
William L. Seymour
Color processing: **COLOR EDGE**
Dino Kairo
Digital scanning and reproduction: **THE SCAN SHOP**
Ebrahim (Bollie) Ganief
Editorial management: **ROELIEN THERON**
Text: Ray Furse
Editing: Roelien Theron, Proofreading: Laurie Rose-Innes, Indexing: Sandie Vahl
Cartographer: Peter Slingsby
Printing and UV spot varnishing: **CREDA COMMUNICATIONS (PTY) LTD**
Roger Austen, Gary Lewis, Mannie Miranda
Binding: **AFRIBIND**
Deon Botha, Werner Botha, Carl le Roux

Published for Eurovast Publications BV by The Gerald & Marc Hoberman Collection (Pty) Ltd
Reg. No. 99/00167/07. PO Box 60044, Victoria Junction, 8005, Cape Town, South Africa
Telephone: 27-21-419 6657/419 2210 Fax: 27-21-418 5987 e-mail: hobercol@mweb.co.za
www.hobermancollection.com

International marketing and picture library

Hoberman Collection (USA), Inc. Representing The Gerald & Marc Hoberman Collection
PO Box 810902, Boca Raton, FL 33481-0902, USA
Telephone: 91-561-542 1141 Fax: 91-864-885 1090 e-mail: hobcolusa@yahoo.com

International inquiries

Eurovast Publications BV, Paradijslaan 70, 4822 PG, Breda, The Netherlands
Telephone: 31-76-541 8815 Fax: 31-76-542 5932 e-mail: eurovast@yahoo.com

Agents and distributors

United States of America,
Canada and Asia:
BHB International, Inc.
108 E. North 1st Street, Suite G
Seneca, SC 29678
Tel: 91-877-242 3266
Fax: 91-864-885 1090
e-mail: bhbbooks@aol.com

United Kingdom and
Republic of Ireland:
John Wilson Booksales
1 High Street, Princes Risborough
Buckinghamshire, HP27 0AG
Tel: 44-1844-275927
Fax: 44-1844-274402
e-mail: sales@jwbs.co.uk

Australia:
Wakefield Press Distribution
Box 2266
Kent Town, SA 5071
Tel: 61-8-8362 8800
Fax: 61-8-8362 7592
e-mail: sales@wakefieldpress.com.au

Germany:
Felix Moehrke
Wilhelmstr. 63
68259, Mannheim
Tel: 49-621-79 00 318
Fax: 49-621-79 00 319
e-mail: info@magmark.de

Namibia:
Projects & Promotions cc
P.O. Box 96102
Windhoek
Tel: 264-61-255715/6
Fax: 264-61-230033
e-mail: proprom@iafrica.com.na

Printed in South Africa

ACKNOWLEDGEMENTS

New York author and Editorial Director of Weatherhill, Inc., Ray Furse is as passionate about his city as we are. His entertaining writing style, meticulous research, and succinct and fascinating text are precisely what we had in mind at the outset to augment our photography. Ray's assistance in driving us to less accessible places, seeking permissions, and dispensing invaluable advice, always with enthusiasm and alacrity, proved invaluable. For his sterling contribution, we are most grateful.

For suggesting we do a book on New York and for introducing us to Ray, we are indebted to Barbara Brackett, President of BHB International, Inc., our distributor and agent in the United States. We are deeply appreciative of her enthusiastic support, as well as that of her daughter Beverley and son Charles, and their network of dedicated representatives.

To our editor extraordinaire, Roelien Theron, who has been associated with our publications since our first book in the series, we remain ever grateful for her perpetual dedication to excellence.

We wish to thank the many organizations and individuals who helped to make this book possible, especially Allison Ellner-Teitelbaum, Executive Director, and Hallie Brown, Public Relations and Marketing Assistant, Broadway Dance Studio; Judy McMillan, Director of Education, Historic Richmond Town; Herbert Scher, Deputy Manager of Public Relations, the New York Public Library; Cecile Archibald and Francine Bellapianta, New York Stock Exchange; Leo F. Spellman, Director of Advertising and Public Relations, Steinway & Sons; Aaron W. Gross and Richard A. Gould, Aron Streit, Inc.; and Louis, Salvatore, and Marie DiPalo of DiPalo's Fine Foods.

GERALD & MARC HOBERMAN

NEW YORK

Riverdale
Hudson River
Kingsbridge
Henry Hudson Bridge
Co-op City
Bronx
Upper Manhattan
George Washington Bridge
Washington Heights
Washington Bridge
Fordham
BRONX ZOO
Bronx Park
Hart Island
Long Island Sound
Parkchester
CROSS BRONX EXPWY
HUTCHINSON RIVER PKWY
THROGS NECK EXPWY
City Island
Highbridge
Tremont
YANKEE STADIUM
WESTCHESTER AVE
BRUCKNER EXPWY
Manhattan
The Hub
Hunts Point
Bronx-Whitestone Bridge
Morningside Heights
Harlem
Triborough Bridge
East River
Rikers Island
Flushing
Whitestone
Wards Island
CROSS ISLAND PKWY
Upper West Side
Central Park
Astoria
LA GUARDIA AIRPORT
Union City
Theater District
Upper East Side
Roosevelt Island
Long Island City
Bayside
Alley Pond Park
Lincoln Tunnel
Garment District
Midtown
Queensboro Bridge
Queens Blvd
Flushing Meadow-Corona Park
QUEENS BOTANICAL GARDEN
LONG ISLAND EXPWY
Murray Hill
Chelsea
Queens Midtown Tunnel
BROOKLYN QUEENS EXPWY
VAN WYCK EXPWY
Queens
Gramercy Park
Newark
Greenwich Village
East Village
Greenpoint
Jamaica
GRAND CENTRAL PKWY
Holland Tunnel
Soho
Little Italy
Bushwick
Long Island
Jersey City
Tribeca
China-town
Lower East Side
Williamsburg Bridge
Forest Hills
Williamsburg
JACKIE ROBINSON PKWY
Forest Park
Lower Manhattan
Battery Park City
Seaport
Manhattan Bridge
WOODHAVEN BLVD
Ellis Island
Brooklyn Bridge
Bedford-Stuyvesant
Ozone Park
STATUE OF LIBERTY
Governors Island
Brooklyn Heights
ATLANTIC AVE
ROCKAWAY BLVD
Liberty Island
EASTERN PKWY
East New York
SOUTHERN PKWY
LAURELTON PKWY
Upper New York Bay
Park Slope
PROSPECT EXPWY
BROOKLYN BOTANIC GARDEN
Crown Heights
Prospect Park
ROCKAWAY PKWY
Howard Beach
JOHN F. KENNEDY INTERNATIONAL AIRPORT
SNUG HARBOR
LINDEN BLVD
Flatbush
GOWANUS EXPWY
ST. GEORGE
STATEN ISLAND FERRY
Jamaica Bay
St. George
FOREST AVE
FORT HAMILTON PKWY
OCEAN PKWY
Brooklyn
Gateway National Recreation Area
WILLOWBROOK EXPWY
The Narrows
Bay Ridge
Westerleigh
Borough Park
KINGS HWY
FLATBUSH AVE
STATEN ISLAND EXPWY
Verrazano Narrows Bridge
Gravesend
WEST SHORE EXPWY
Willow Brook Park
Fresh Kill Park
South Beach
Sheepshead Bay
BELT PKWY
Staten Island
HISTORIC RICHMOND TOWN
Richmond Town
HYLAN BLVD
Coney Island
Brighton Beach
Gateway National Recreation Area
New Springville
La Tourette Park
New Dorp
Rockaway Beach
RICHMOND PKWY
Great Kills
Eltingville
Great Kills Park
Gateway National Recreation Area
Lower New York Bay
Breezy Point
Gateway National Recreation Area

N

ATLANTIC OCEAN

Tottenville

0 ——————— 5 miles
0 ——————— 10 km

MANHATTAN

Henry Hudson Bridge
THE CLOISTERS
Upper Manhattan
George Washington Bridge
Washington Bridge
Washington Heights
HENRY HUDSON PKWY
HARLEM RIVER DRIVE
Harlem River
Hamilton Heights
Morningside Heights
CATHEDRAL OF ST. JOHN THE DIVINE
Harlem
Triborough Bridge
Hudson River
Riverside Park
Riverside Hwy
WEST SIDE HWY
Upper West Side
Central Park
MET MUSEUM
GUGGENHEIM
5TH AVE
PARK AVE
FD ROOSEVELT DRIVE
Wards Island
Upper East Side
Roosevelt Island
LINCOLN CENTER
CARNEGIE HALL
BROADWAY
Lincoln Tunnel
Theater District
Midtown
Queensboro Bridge
TIMES SQUARE
ST. PATRICK'S
ROCKEFELLER CENTER
Garment District
GRAND CENTRAL TERMINAL
CHRYSLER BUILDING
CHELSEA PIERS
NY PUBLIC LIBRARY
Murray Hill
UNITED NATIONS
EMPIRE STATE BUILDING
Queens Midtown Tunnel
Chelsea
MADISON SQUARE
Gramercy Park
FLATIRON BUILDING
UNION SQUARE
Holland Tunnel
Greenwich Village
East Village
Soho
Little Italy
Tribeca
China-town
Lower East Side
Civic Center
Williamsburg Bridge
WORLD TRADE CENTER
Lower Manhattan
Battery Park City
Financial District
NYSE
Seaport
Manhattan Bridge
Brooklyn Bridge
Battery Park
Brooklyn-Battery Tunnel
Ellis Island
STATUE OF LIBERTY
Liberty Island
Governors Island

FOREWORD

BY THOMAS SULLIVAN
Deputy Managing Editor, News
New York *Daily News*

That New York is a capital city of finance and commerce, of arts and ideas, is well-known. Gerald and Marc Hoberman's New York *presents the city as a visual capital—stunning and soothing, arrogant and humble.*

The photographs are taken at ground level and from high above the skyscrapers to offer different perspectives on a widely varying landscape, from wall graffiti announcing the start of baseball's "Subway Series" to extraordinary aerial views of the city's latticework of bridges.

The reader comes to see New York as a repository of history, but also an organic life-force capable of constantly reinventing itself, as in the Chelsea Piers, once a busy shipping area, now a popular indoor and outdoor recreation center. There are photographs of buildings that are synonymous with New York—the Empire State, the Chrysler, the Flatiron, and Grand Central—spectacular structures, beautifully depicted. The images portray as well the new arising amid the old, and the juxtaposition of the colonial and the modern; for example, the ventilation tower for the Brooklyn-Battery Tunnel rising out of New York Bay next to Fort Jay on Governors Island, built to protect the city against seaborne invaders.

New York's reputation for high living is confirmed by photographs of the Russian Tea Room and the 21 Club and contrasted with the homey atmosphere of DiPalo's Fine Foods in Little Italy and the Victory Diner on Staten Island.

The Hobermans' New York *portrays the city as destination, a role it has played for centuries, from gateway to the New World—via Ellis Island—to the dream city for the fulfillment of artistic aspirations, as symbolized in the images of the hard-working performers at the Broadway Dance Center. The photographs also reflect the New*

World's promise of freedom of religious expression: penniless immigrants prosper and build imposing monuments to their faith, such as St. Patrick's Cathedral and Temple Emanu-El.

New York is itself a temple of wealth and art, a place where the two often merge through the vision of the world's most accomplished architects, such as Frank Lloyd Wright's design for the Solomon R. Guggenheim Museum. Performing arts also converge at Carnegie Hall and Lincoln Center's palaces of music, dance, and theater.

And there are the architects of everyday life who make the city work: police, stock exchange messengers, fish market workers, and fruit and vegetable vendors. The Hobermans present the city's varied faces, residents who can trace their origins from every corner of the earth, the privileged and the marginal, the famous and the obscure. The city is also their playground, as the photographs attest—New Yorkers jogging in Central Park, skating at Rockefeller Center, strolling in Flushing Meadow-Corona Park, and sunning themselves at Coney Island.

The Hobermans' New York *captures life in the city, old and new, open and hidden. Its stunning images and insightful commentary are both an informative introduction for the newcomer and a delight to the native, those of us who note and record the ever-changing pace and daily life of New York City.*

Thomas Sullivan

THOMAS SULLIVAN
New York 2001

INTRODUCTION

Gigantic golden towers scintillate in the early light of dawn. The heaven-kissing monoliths of Manhattan rise from a ballast of bedrock. Skyscrapers, some with decorative spires, vie with each other to be the loftiest, cloud-touching pinnacle in the city. Steel, chrome, aluminum, brick, marble, and brownstone buildings sit foursquare, resolute as a New York deal. After dark the New York skyline lights up and owns the night.

New York City—perpetually pulsating, vibrant, innovative, abrupt, brash, caring, and cultured. Liberty is her lady, Ellis Island her historic portal of freedom, and the mighty Hudson her river.

Central Park in spring is green, lush, and leafy; in fall, bedecked with burnished browns and russet hues; in winter, crisp and icy. Here the mainspring that makes New York tick unwinds as the world watches. It is a place to daydream, romance, stroll, jog, rollerblade, cycle, row, fish, ice-skate, ride sedately in a horse-drawn carriage, play baseball or basketball, engage in an intense game of chess, sail a model boat on a tranquil pond, or perhaps sit on a bench watching the world go by.

New York is linked to the world by spectacular bridges, tunnels, toll roads, railroads, and airports, and there is an ever-constant flow of humanity, enhanced by the spice of ethnicity and cultural diversity. It is a world within a world, a city without equal.

We took to the skies over New York in a helicopter, our cameras at the ready. It was a rare sunny December day, with crystal clear, cobalt-blue skies, near-freezing temperatures, and the long shadows of

GERALD HOBERMAN

MARC HOBERMAN

early morning accentuating the scenic splendor. We soared over the tallest skyscrapers and swooped low over the many bridges and tunnels of New York, marveling at the variety and ingenuity of their design and construction.

We were awed by the beauty of the Statue of Liberty from the air, her verdant patina iridescing in the light of early dawn. Cradling a tablet in one hand, inscribed in roman numerals with July 4, 1776, the date of America's Declaration of Independence, and holding her torch aloft, its flame of gold glinting as if on fire, she seemed to gaze like an ancient Greek goddess across the water towards the Manhattan skyline—every side of her classic symmetry equally photogenic.

Back down on earth, so to speak, we covered the length and breadth of New York, returning in the spring in pursuit of the city's essence.

We are most fortunate to have had the privilege to experience the wonders and excitement of New York. Through our photography, illuminated by the informative and fascinating text of native New Yorker Ray Furse, we are delighted to be able to share our experiences and perspective on this great city and its attributes with you.

Gerald Hoberman

M Hoberman

GERALD & MARC HOBERMAN
New York 2001

THE CITY OF HURRIED AND SPARKLING WATERS! THE CITY OF SPIRES AND MASTS!
THE CITY NESTED IN BAYS! MY CITY!

WALT WHITMAN (1819–1892)

The word "skyscraper" comes from nautical slang; it was the term sailors used for the tallest mast of a sailing ship. Although New York was not the first to use this construction technique, building tall has been a local tradition since the late nineteenth century. On the practical side, individual plots of land, a relic of colonial times, were small, and not always suitable for the placement of wide-based buildings. More importantly, though, height confers prestige, and having grand headquarters in America's center for trade with the world was evidence of a corporation's economic might.

Today New York's major buildings—the Empire State Building, the World Trade Center, and the Chrysler Building seen here—are among the most recognized structures in the world, and the city displays the widest variety of skyscraper architectural styles to be seen anywhere.

STARTING THE DAY, SOUTH STREET SEAPORT

The great metropolis of New York City is a hodgepodge of cultures, making the rituals of its inhabitants myriad and endlessly fascinating. Somewhere in the city are people enjoying rice and fish for breakfast while their neighbors are preparing bacon and eggs. Here at the South Street Seaport, in the shadow of the Brooklyn Bridge, a businessman enjoys a break before work by perusing the morning newspaper. His unnoticed neighbor further down the boardwalk engages in t'ai chi ch'uan, a soft martial art that is popularly practiced by Chinese in the morning. It is supposed to activate the flow of *ch'i*, believed to be the vital universal force that animates all living things.

WEST SIDE PASSENGER TERMINAL

Travelers up the Hudson River should be forgiven for imagining that a new, white skyscraper had been added to the western Manhattan skyline. What they might be seeing instead is the stern of the 85,000-ton *Costa Atlantica*, the newest flagship of the Costa cruise line. With a crew and staff of 920 and a guest capacity of 2100, the liner could indeed be considered a new luxury hotel. Although New York Harbor does not have anywhere near the passenger liner traffic it enjoyed during the heyday of transatlantic ship travel, city residents still have many cruise opportunities: in winter ships depart for the Caribbean and in spring they leave for the Mediterranean.

FULTON FISH MARKET

Wholesalers have purchased fresh fish for resale to stores, restaurants, and fish lovers at this Lower East Side location for almost two centuries. The first fishmongers to set up here in 1822 sold their wares from makeshift stalls; those were replaced in 1869 by a permanent building. By the end of the century, improved transport and the invention of refrigeration allowed fish to be shipped all over the country, and Fulton Fish Market became the largest fish market in the world. In those days, fishing boats would navigate up the East River to dock at the market, where they would unload their catch; today fish is delivered by truck from piers up and down the coast and from local airports, where it is flown in from the west coast and many foreign countries. Now that modern air transport facilitates delivery of seafood directly from fishery to marketplace, Fulton Fish Market does not enjoy nearly the volume of business it once did. Still, a strong local market and the availability of specialty items from around the world make it the nation's premier fish market.

A WORKING WATERFRONT

Just after midnight, when most New Yorkers have turned in for the night, refrigerated trucks from all over the country and small vans from local restaurants rumble down Front Street to the Fulton Fish Market, where they deliver or load up fresh seafood from around the world. Unloading, selling, and loading continue throughout the night, ending at around nine in the morning. Unfortunately, this last vestige of a working waterfront and last great open-air market in Manhattan is scheduled to disappear; plans are underway to move it to a new facility in the Bronx, near Hunts Point Terminal, the largest produce market in the world.

SOUTH STREET SEAPORT

This historic port area was the center of New York's shipping trade from the early 1800s until the Civil War, when cargo ships grew much larger and began to use facilities elsewhere. The South Street Seaport sank into general seediness until it was restored as a tourist area in the late 1960s. Among its many attractions is the vintage ship, the *Peking*. Built in Hamburg, Germany, in 1911, the four-masted barque was used to carry cargo from Europe to South America. At 377 feet long and weighing 3100 gross tons, she is one of the largest sailing vessels ever built, and one of the last of the great era of wind-powered vessels.

BATTERY PARK CITY

On the lower west side of Manhattan adjacent to Battery Park, this vast commercial and residential complex occupies 92 acres, over a quarter of which is landfill resulting from excavation for the World Trade Center (one of the two towers is shown at the upper left). The complex was developed by a public benefit corporation established in 1968. The landfill was not completed until 1976, just before a city-wide fiscal crisis halted all construction. In spite of that sluggish start, however, the complex today is hugely successful, with a lovely esplanade along the Hudson River linking restaurants, public spaces, and artworks, making it a popular destination for a summer weekend.

CHRYSLER BUILDING

The energy, industrial, and transportation tycoons of the nineteenth and early twentieth centuries left their names on many buildings and public works, both in New York City and across America. Everywhere one turns in the city, names like Carnegie (steel), Rockefeller (oil), and Vanderbilt (railroads) are encountered. Yet nothing changed American life as profoundly as the automobile, and among the great pioneers in this industry was Walter Percy Chrysler. Born in Wamego, Kansas, in 1875, he was first a railroad mechanic before heading out at the age of 22 to seek his fortune. He worked for several car companies, including General Motors, before founding his own company. In 1924 Chrysler unveiled the first vehicle bearing the Chrysler name in New York City. He was barred from presenting it at the New York Auto Show because it was not available for sale yet, so he displayed his "Chrysler Six" in the lobby of the nearby Hotel Commodore. The powerful and fast (an unheard-of 70 miles per hour) new model caused a media and industry sensation, and sold almost 32,000 units, the largest number ever for a new American launch. Six years later the Chrysler Building, the world's tallest, was completed at 42nd Street and Lexington Avenue.

Chrysler has now merged with Daimler of Germany to create one of the world's largest automotive manufacturers, DaimlerChrysler, with annual revenues totaling more than $160 billion. It employs over 400,000 people in 37 countries to make nearly five million vehicles a year.

In 1941 President Franklin D. Roosevelt coined the term "United Nations" to describe the allied countries opposing Germany and the other Axis powers during World War II. The Moscow Declaration of 1943 made official the desire of the United States of America, the Union of Soviet Socialist Republics (USSR), China, and Great Britain to create a new international organization to facilitate peace and diplomacy. The United Nations charter was ratified in San Francisco two years later, on October 24, now officially United Nations Day.

Although the General Assembly first met in London in January of 1946, it was decided to build a headquarters for the new organization in New York City on an $8.5-million tract of land along the East River donated by John D. Rockefeller, Jr. The main buildings of the complex, completed in 1952, are the General Assembly, the Conference Building, and the Secretariat (seen here), a 39-story office tower accommodating 3400 employees.

Although the United Nations has not achieved the world peace that many idealists had hoped it would, it has successfully intervened in a number of crises to end or avert escalating conflict. United Nations Peacekeeping Forces today stand between warring countries at practically all international trouble spots we read about in the news every day.

GRAND CENTRAL TERMINAL

New Yorkers love to correct those hapless visitors who call this depot Grand Central Station. "It's Grand Central *Terminal*," they say, "because the trains *end* here!" Built in 1913 for the unheard-of sum of $43 million, it replaced the old depot of the New York Central Railroad, which was plagued by congestion and the smoke of steam engines. The new facility featured two levels of tracks with electrified third rails. Sadly, the golden age of rail travel has ended, and all long-distance trains, run by Amtrak, depart from the subterranean cavern of Penn Station. Still, Grand Central Terminal thrives; nearly 70 million local commuters pass through it each year.

MAIN CONCOURSE, GRAND CENTRAL TERMINAL

In 1968 Grand Central Terminal was scheduled to be torn down to make way for a 70-story office tower. A public outcry ensued and preservationists, supported by Jackie Kennedy, successfully fought to save it. It is now designated a historic monument, and a recent massive renovation has returned it to its original splendor. All the marble has been polished, the fixtures repaired, and the huge, heavenly vault of the ceiling, painted with constellations, has been cleaned. New shops and restaurants have opened in its several concourses, and visitors delight in strolling through and shopping, even if they are not taking a train anywhere. Grand Central Terminal is once again grand.

AN ENGINEERING MARVEL

When completed in 1883, the Brooklyn Bridge was the longest suspension bridge in the world, the first to be built of steel, and the second tallest structure (after Trinity Church) in the city. Although still remembered as an engineering marvel of its day, what continues to impress is its beauty; its intricate cabling appears spun in gossamer strands between its massive Gothic towers. This was the end of the nineteenth century, before the automobile was in use. A trip from New York to Brooklyn (then a separate city, the third largest in America) meant a leisurely buggy ride or a pleasant stroll along a promenade that soared high above the busy East River below.

The 1350-foot twin towers of the World Trade Center now rank with the Statue of Liberty and the Empire State Building as icons representing New York City and its majestic skyline. Rising from reclaimed land once covered by the Hudson River, they are engineering wonders as well. Unlike typical skyscrapers, whose walls are "hung" on steel skeletons, the walls of the World Trade Center towers are load-bearing; the only steel columns within the buildings are components of the 104 elevator shafts. This design maximizes the interior area—there is an acre of rentable space on each floor—but severely limits the size and number of windows.

The entire complex, which includes four more smaller buildings, is used by 50,000 workers and receives up to 100,000 visitors each day, most of whom flock to the huge underground shopping arcade or the 107th-floor observation deck. Still, the center has never been beloved by some New York natives, who regard the complex as cold and unadorned. Yet, a touch of golden sunlight on these twin towers at dawn paints an indelible picture.

THE FINANCIAL DISTRICT

Guarding the northern entrance to Bowling Green is a 3.3-ton bronze bull, installed in 1988. Pawing the ground with its head lowered, the bull appears ready to charge through the Financial District to the north. The origin of "bulls and bears" as symbols of a rising and falling stock market dates back to eighteenth-century New York. "Bearskin jobbers" were speculators who promised delivery of a stock they did not own, in expectation that the price would fall—the term derives from a popular expression, "to sell the bearskin before you catch the bear." Bulls were regarded as the bears' natural antagonists, so "bulls and bears" came into popular usage.

TAKING A WELL-EARNED BREAK

It is doubtful that even founding father George Washington, whose statue stands on the steps of Federal Hall in the distance, could have envisioned the consequences of New York's central role in the financial life of the nation. Even before the American revolution, the wall that once stood here to protect residents from attack was torn down to make way for the city's surging expansion. The thoroughfare mapped out in its place, Wall Street, became home to banks, shippers, and insurance companies, and went on to become the commercial center of the city and the country. Stocks and bonds, the latter mostly issued by the government, were bought and sold like bales of cotton or casks of sugar, by brokers in competitive bidding. The Buttonwood Agreement of 1792, to which the New York Stock Exchange dates its origins, simply consolidated the rules of the game. The rest, as they say, is history.

After two centuries of growth and innovation, the New York Stock Exchange remains the world's foremost securities marketplace, raising more capital than any other market in the world. More than 2900 companies are listed on the exchange, whose combined 315 billion shares available for trading are worth more than $12 trillion in total global market capitalization, more than three times that of any other market. Here stock exchange employees take a break from work, which, on an average day, includes trading more than a billion shares worth more than $40 billion.

NEW YORK STOCK EXCHANGE

All stock exchanges rely on the premise that at any given time there are people who want to buy and sell a certain stock, let's say shares of Enterprise, Inc. When John Smith instructs his broker to buy ten shares of Enterprise, his order is sent electronically to the trading floor. There a floor broker represents the order, conveying it either in printed form or by wireless voice or data terminal to the trading crowd. Smith's broker and another floor broker representing a seller agree on a price; in doing so, they are competing with other buyers and sellers, so that the fairest possible price is obtained for both sides. When the transaction is agreed upon, it is reported to a specific trading post, where a specialist in charge of Enterprise stock makes sure that the trade is executed properly and is reported both to the brokerage firms who initiated the buy and sell orders and to the "consolidated tape," the electronic reporting system that displays prices and trades across the country and around the world.

The New York Stock Exchange is in essence a customer-oriented, two-way auction market, where transactions take place through an open presentation of bids and offers made by brokers on behalf of their customers. This open-market auction system assures investors narrower spreads, better liquidity, and fairer prices.

THE TRADING FLOOR

Visitors should not be fooled by the Classical Revival façade of the New York Stock Exchange's 1903 building; the main trading floor has been renovated and updated to facilitate the swift flow and display of massive amounts of information and an ever-increasing trading capacity. A tubular steel frame suspended above the floor carries lines distributing power and information to the main trading posts below (marked by the blue NYSE signs), allowing the volume of a full day of trading ten years ago to be accommodated in fifteen minutes today.

Although the New York Stock Exchange was not formally established until 1817, when a group of brokers adopted a constitution and set up formal membership rules, the organization traces its origins back to the historic Buttonwood Agreement of 1792. That pact, in which 24 New York merchants and stockbrokers agreed on uniform commissions and rules to prevent monopolistic trading, was so named because it was signed out-of-doors, under a buttonwood tree where the group often met. When weather was inclement, they supposedly repaired to the nearby Tontine Coffee House. After the New York Stock Exchange was officially established, it was housed in a rented room at 40 Wall Street.

The facilities have come a long way since then. In 1865 a five-story building was opened at 10 Broad Street, which was successively enlarged and remodeled, until demolished in 1901 to make way for the current building at Broad and Wall Streets. It was designed in the Classical Revival style by well-known architect and engineer George B. Post. The pediment, designed by sculptor John Quincy Adams Ward, features a central figure symbolizing integrity, flanked by ten other figures representing sources of wealth, including industry, invention, agriculture, mining, and science.

"…easy is the sleep of Alexander Hamilton. / …easy is the sleep of Robert Fulton. / …easy are the great governments and the great steamboats." So ends the poem "Trinity Place," by the American poet Carl Sandburg, which reflects the ironic location of Trinity Church—established by the charter of King William III of England in 1697—where Broadway meets Wall Street. The latter, of course, has always been an engine of economic and technological progress in America, while the church has historically ministered to the needs of the city's disadvantaged. The city's first ministry to African-Americans, both enslaved and free, began at Trinity in 1705, while during both the nineteenth and twentieth centuries, Trinity offered assistance to successive waves of immigrants who poured into New York.

Meanwhile, in Trinity's graveyard lie Alexander Hamilton, revolutionary leader, founder of the Bank of New York, and first Secretary of the Treasury, and Robert Fulton, developer of the world's first commercially successful passenger steamboat, which ranks with the invention of the microchip as a milestone of technological advancement.

These men, foremost among those responsible for making the United States the great power it is today, both died in New York City. They were laid to rest in the quiet yard of Trinity Church, where, as Sandburg noted, "stenogs, bundle boys, scrub-women, sit on the tombstones and walk on the grass of graves, speaking of war and weather, of babies, wages and love."

FEDERAL HALL NATIONAL MEMORIAL

The first structure erected on this site was the colony of New York's City Hall, built in 1699. General George Washington was sworn in as the nation's first president here on April 30, 1789; a statue commemorating the event stands on the steps. New York City was then the nation's capital, but when the seat of government moved to Philadelphia in 1790, the building again became City Hall, until it was demolished in 1812. In the 1830s, the United States Custom House, a fine example of Greek Revival architecture, was built here. Due to the rich history of the site, it is now designated the Federal Hall National Memorial.

HORSE-DRAWN CARRIAGE, CENTRAL PARK

In 1831 the omnibus, a horse-drawn carriage for public transport, was introduced in New York. From then until the latter part of the century, when cable-drawn and electric streetcars were introduced, New York City was the leading manufacturer of horse-drawn vehicles in America. Although now in use only around the Theater District and midtown, horse-drawn carriages are still popular, especially for romantic evening rides through Central Park.

SPRING FLOWERS, GRAND ARMY PLAZA

"I found it exceedingly pleasant to walk in the town, for it seemed quite like a garden." So wrote the Swedish naturalist Peter Kalm about his 1748 visit to Manhattan. Kalm was the first European naturalist to collect and study the plants and animals of North America; the English translation of his journals was published as *Travels in North America* in 1770–71 in three volumes. His specimens were sent to the great botanical cataloger Linnaeus, who graciously named a genus of flowering shrub, the mountain laurel (*Kalmia latifolia*), after his friend. This large and brightly flowered square is part of Grand Army Plaza, site of the Plaza Hotel and the main gateway to Central Park.

NEWLYWEDS, GRAND ARMY PLAZA

Nearly 40 million people visit New York City each year, twenty percent of them from abroad. A million come from the United Kingdom alone, followed by Canada, Germany, and Japan. Some just come for the sightseeing, while others, obviously, have other agendas. Here at the appropriately romantic Grand Army Plaza, these newlyweds record an important milestone in their romance, while another tourist, who has seen enough sights for the afternoon, blissfully snoozes nearby.

CENTRAL PARK—AN URBAN OASIS

Looking south from northern Manhattan, it is easy to see why Central Park is called "the lungs of the city." By the mid-nineteenth century it was clear that development would ultimately engulf Manhattan and that a city park was desperately needed. In 1856 the city purchased for $5 million what was then a desolate stretch of property (now central Manhattan between 59th and 110th Streets), occupied by a garbage dump and the pigs and goats of squatters. Today this great park is one of the urban wonders of the world, a green oasis in the great concrete, high-rise landscape of the city.

THE CREATION OF CENTRAL PARK

Although this grand city park appears to be the last vestige of natural land in an otherwise asphalt-coated cityscape, the 843 acres of Central Park were in fact completely landscaped. After the city purchased the land, it held a competition for the creation of a park. It was won by Frederick Law Olmsted and his partner Calvert Vaux, whose plan called for enhancing the land's natural irregularities. To accomplish this, workers covered an initial layer of ten million cartloads of earth with half a million cubic yards of topsoil, then planted nearly five million trees of 632 species, plus 815 varieties of plants.

A PARK OF PLEASURE

It is easy to see why the real estate of Central Park West and Fifth Avenue, which border Central Park on the west and east respectively, commands such astronomical prices. In addition to enjoying fabulous views and fresher air, residents can participate in a wide variety of activities. In addition to the usual recreational outlets—biking, running, and ball games—the park offers classes in yoga, t'ai chi ch'uan, bird watching, and even cross-country skiing. And for those whose workweek has left them totally drained, there is always the world's most popular sport—people watching.

CENTRAL PARK—A HAVEN FOR SPORTS ENTHUSIASTS

A paradise for sports-loving men and women, Central Park offers an incredible variety of recreational activities. Joggers and bladers can enjoy both hilly and flat terrain. A favorite for runners is the 1.58-mile loop round the Jacqueline Kennedy Onassis Reservoir, offering outstanding skyline views and natural scenery; a bonus in spring are the blooming cherry trees. Circling the entire park are various drives suitable for runners, cyclists, and rollerbladers (auto traffic is banned on weekends). There are also three linked, soft-surface bridle trails. Truly serious sports enthusiasts should take note that Central Park is the site of the final 3.2 miles of the annual New York Marathon.

GREAT LAWN

The Great Lawn was not included in the original plan for Central Park. The site was then occupied by a 33-acre reservoir for the city's drinking water, and the park had to be planned around it. When the reservoir became obsolete, it was filled, in part, with excavated material from Rockefeller Center, then being built to the south. Today the Great Lawn features fields and courts for softball, soccer, basketball, and volleyball. It has also hosted some of the city's biggest public events, from a Paul Simon concert to a papal mass. Both the New York Philharmonic and the Metropolitan Opera give two free performances here on summer nights.

BASEBALL GAME, CENTRAL PARK

Although the precise circumstances of baseball's invention are unclear, the sport's early association with New York City is not in doubt. The rules for a "New York Game" were published in 1846 by the Knickerbocker Club, a group of Manhattanites who played ball on a field where Madison Square stands today. (The first contest officially conducted under the new rules was played in Hoboken, New Jersey). But even without this association, New York's contribution to baseball tradition rests secure: New York fans were the first to eat hot dogs at a ball park and the first to hear *Take Me Out to the Ball Game*, a song written by two New Yorkers.

BASKETBALL GAME, CENTRAL PARK

Although the modern game of basketball was invented in 1891 in Springfield, Massachusetts, New York City is widely acknowledged as the center of basketball during its formative years. The game caught on rapidly and by the turn of the century was being played throughout the city in schools, clubs, and YMCAs. The first professional team, the New York Celtics, was formed here in 1914, and New York City colleges—notably City College, New York University, and St. John's—dominated the sport at that level. A college basketball scholarship is still considered a sure ticket to success.

This is Manhattan? City dwellers spend a good deal of time pondering the problem of how to get away from it all without going too far, and Central Park provides numerous solutions. After the reservoir, which is not used for recreation and is soon to be closed, The Lake is Central Park's largest body of water, and was created by park designers Frederick Law Olmsted and Calvert Vaux out of a swamp. Although only 22 acres, its undulating shoreline makes it seem much larger, and boaters come to explore its many turns and delight in its varied views. During the nineteenth century, visitors to the park enjoyed the services of six-seater "call boats," which operated like water taxis, or larger canopied boats, which took them around the entire lake, stopping at five boat landings where they could embark or disembark, for a dime. Those days of Victorian gentility are gone; today's boaters usually row themselves, in small boats rented from Loeb Boathouse, although a few gondolas still carry passengers.

The years of the park's construction, in the late 1850s, saw a series of extremely cold winters, during which the frozen lake was opened to the public for ice-skating, an event deemed responsible for turning the sport into a New York craze. As many as 40,000 people used to skate here in a single day.

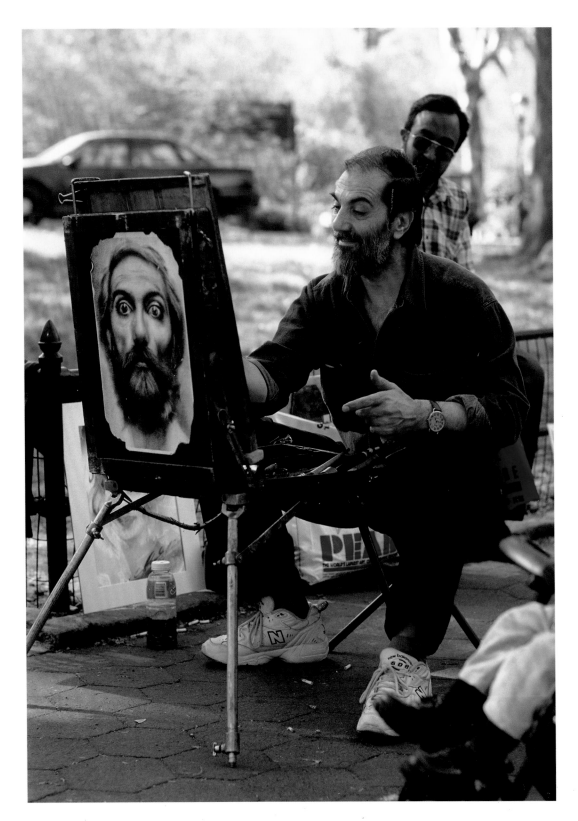

PORTRAIT ARTIST, CENTRAL PARK

New York City is to art in America as Paris is to art on the Continent: it is the place where, if you "make it," your reputation in the art world is assured. Throughout the eighteenth century, American artists usually earned a living by painting portraits of the rich and powerful. By the mid-nineteenth century the invention of photography had reduced that demand, and painters increasingly turned their attention to landscape; the works of a group of artists known as the Hudson River School were immensely popular.

New York City has always been at the forefront of new art movements. The Armory Show of 1913, featuring the Dadaism of Marcel Duchamp and photographer Man Ray, introduced modern art to America. The abstraction and surrealism of the 1930s and 40s is seen in the works of such artists as Hans Hoffman and Max Ernst, who with others were known as the New York School, and led to the abstract expressionism of Jackson Pollock and Willem de Kooning. Postwar trends have been diverse and include the preoccupation with popular culture, evident in the works of Jasper Johns and Robert Rauschenberg, and in the pop art of the 1960s, such as Roy Lichtenstein's giant comic book panels and Andy Warhol's celebration of the soup can. Still, new trends may come and go, but as long as art strives to represent life, traditional modes of presentation will endure, as seen by this portrait artist plying his trade in Central Park.

SHEEP MEADOW

This 22-acre clearing on the west side of Central Park was originally incorporated into the design of the park in compliance with a rule that there must be a place for soldiers to drill. After that stipulation was dropped, sheep did indeed graze here for nearly six decades. In 1934, parks commissioner Robert Moses evicted the sheep and converted the former sheepfold into Tavern on the Green, which remains an immensely popular restaurant. Although formerly sports and recreational activities were allowed, today Sheep Meadow is reserved for quiet picnicking, reading, and relaxing, and on most sunny weekends is the most popular spot in the park.

STATUE OF ALICE IN WONDERLAND

A favorite destination for children visiting Central Park is José de Creeft's tableau of the beloved characters from Lewis Carroll's *Alice in Wonderland*. Alice perches on the largest of a group of mushrooms, while the March Hare examines his pocket watch and frets about the time, the Dormouse nibbles on a snack, the Cheshire Cat catches Alice's eye, and the Mad Hatter ponders his own vision of reality. Nearby, a statue of Hans Christian Andersen by Georg John Lober shows the master of fairy tales sitting on a bench with a book spread open on his legs, as if inviting children to come and listen to a story.

CONSERVATORY WATER

This pond in Central Park takes its name from the original plan of park designers Frederick Law Olmsted and Calvert Vaux to build a huge conservatory on the site. When budget constraints made that impossible, they borrowed the idea of a model boat pond, popular in Paris in the late nineteenth century. Today both children and adults come to test and race their own model boats, or they may rent a vessel from nearby vendors. A Model Yacht Club, headquartered in the Kerbs Boathouse seen behind the pond, organizes regular regattas featuring radio-controlled model boats.

FISHING AT HARLEM MEER

Although at only 11 acres, this quiet lake in the northeast corner of Central Park is not the "small sea" that the word *meer* means in Dutch, it is nonetheless a popular neighborhood attraction. Harlem Meer is stocked with largemouth bass, channel catfish, bluegill, and pumpkinseed sunfish. Grass carp were added because they eat the algae that can sometimes cloud the water during warm weather. Anglers who come to try their luck abide by the rule of "catch and release." Across the lake stands the Charles A. Dana Discovery Center, the park's only environmental educational center to host children's workshops year-round.

THE DAIRY, CENTRAL PARK

The Dairy is an odd structure, with Gothic touches on what might have been a Swiss chalet. Many visitors assume that the name and design of this little building, which houses the Visitor Center, are simply concessions to a quaint rusticity appropriate for its surroundings. In fact, it was actually designed as a dairy, a place where families could get a fresh drink of milk after their long trek to the park, at a time when settled Manhattan ended two miles to the south, at 38th Street. It was also an era of tainted milk and cholera epidemics, so the fresh, dependably regulated milk sold here was a welcome treat.

WOLLMAN RINK

The Wollman Rink opened in 1949 and has been a solid success ever since; over 300,000 skaters used it during its first year of operation, and today over 4000 come daily. The rink is situated between the Dairy to the north and the Pond to the south, creating a picturesque rural scene that is improbably framed by the high-rise buildings sprouting from the trees in the distance. Under a full moon, against the backdrop of twinkling apartment lights, skaters and visitors alike are treated to one of the world's most romantic skylines.

Central Park is closed to motorized traffic on weekends, when it presents a colorful panorama of New Yorkers at play. Nearly twenty million people visit the park annually, to jog, bike, or rollerblade around a 7-mile main circuit, play tennis, swim, race model boats, ride the carousel, hear a concert, enjoy Shakespeare on a summer night, lie in the sun at Sheep Meadow, or simply enjoy a sedate stroll. Whatever the level of activity, it is a place where all city dwellers can alter the rhythms of their daily urban routines, and emerge refreshed.

As you walk along, you may have a feeling of *déjà vu*; even if you are a first-time visitor, the park somehow seems familiar. Perhaps you saw the movie *Romeo and Juliet*, filmed in the park in 1908. Or perhaps it was *Breakfast at Tiffany's* (1961) or *Love Story* (1970) or *The Way We Were* (1973) or *Hair* (1979) or *Tootsie* (1983) or *Fatal Attraction* (1987) or *Wall Street* (1987), or another of the more than 140 movies containing scenes filmed in Central Park. When you study these scenes carefully, you will notice that not much real action takes place, but rather a lot of talking, arguing, and working out of issues. This is Central Park, the contemplative heart of New York, with nature as friend, adviser, and counselor.

SIDEWALK SANTA

In 1897 Virginia O'Hanlon, age eight, wrote to *The New York Sun*: "Some of my little friends say there is no Santa Claus. Papa says, 'If you see it in *The Sun*, it's so.' Please tell me the truth, is there a Santa Claus?" Her letter found its way into the hands of Francis P. Church, whose reply in the editorial page of the paper was an immediate sensation, and became one of the most famous editorials ever written. Church replied: "Yes, Virginia, there is a Santa Claus. He exists as certainly as love and generosity and devotion exist, and you know that they abound and give to your life its highest beauty and joy."

CITY OF CONTRASTS

The denseness of the urban environment often seems to magnify differences between people—their dress, their jobs, their lives, and their livelihoods. As one of the world's largest and most diverse cities, New York provides endless studies in contrast, often between the rich and poor. Unfortunately, America's tide of prosperity of the last decade has not raised all boats. While the average income of the richest fifth of families increased between the late 1970s and the mid-1990s, the average income of the poorest fifth declined. Here on Fifth Avenue, a "stretch limo" whizzing by while a Salvation Army soldier collects for the poor, highlights this disparity.

Bounded by 48th and 51st Streets and extending west from Fifth Avenue, Rockefeller Center remains perhaps the most imposing example in New York of a modernist skyscraper complex. Embellished with Art Deco details, it successfully fuses public and private, commercial and entertainment spaces. Although access is available from all sides, most visitors turn off Fifth Avenue on to the Channel Gardens, so named because they lie between the British Empire Building and La Maison Française. This short walkway through the gardens with its fountains and granite pools is always attractively planted, with wintertime given over to Christmas decorations highlighting the great tree and skating rink ahead.

At the center of the complex stands the General Electric Building, at 850 feet its tallest building. The General Electric Corporation is now the parent company of RCA (Radio Corporation of America), the original tenant and owner of NBC (National Broadcasting Company). At one time all of the radio programming of this giant network originated here, and the more popular name for Rockefeller Center was "Radio City."

The "Radio City" project that was eventually to become Rockefeller Center was officially unveiled to the press in March of 1931 amid a flurry of publicity. Reviewers were not kind; the plan was called both "weakly conceived" and "a cross-section of metropolitan disorder." Time has proved those critics wrong, and even the great Swiss architect Le Corbusier pronounced the complex "harmonious in its functional elements." By concentrating so much office space in a single tower, architects, led by Raymond Hood, could keep the buildings fronting Fifth Avenue low and attractive, thereby assuring enough light and air to make the surrounding environment pleasant.

The only initial design failure was the sunken plaza in front of the former RCA Building. It could never attract enough visitors and thus never support the planned retail tenants. However, with the advent of new refrigeration technology, it was decided to experiment and turn the plaza into a skating rink in the winter months (in the summer it serves as an outdoor café), a plan that succeeded brilliantly. Above the rink every Christmas season soars a huge tree—its minimum height is 65 feet—with more than 25,000 lights, keeping alive a tradition that began back in 1931, when workers building the center erected a 20-foot Christmas tree on the construction site. Together the rink and tree have made the center an enormously popular wintertime tourist destination.

In addition to its outstanding artwork, skating rink, and Christmas tree, Rockefeller Center attracts visitors to the shops, restaurants, and other services of its vast underground concourses. Besides the 60,000 people who work there, it is visited daily by nearly 200,000 more.

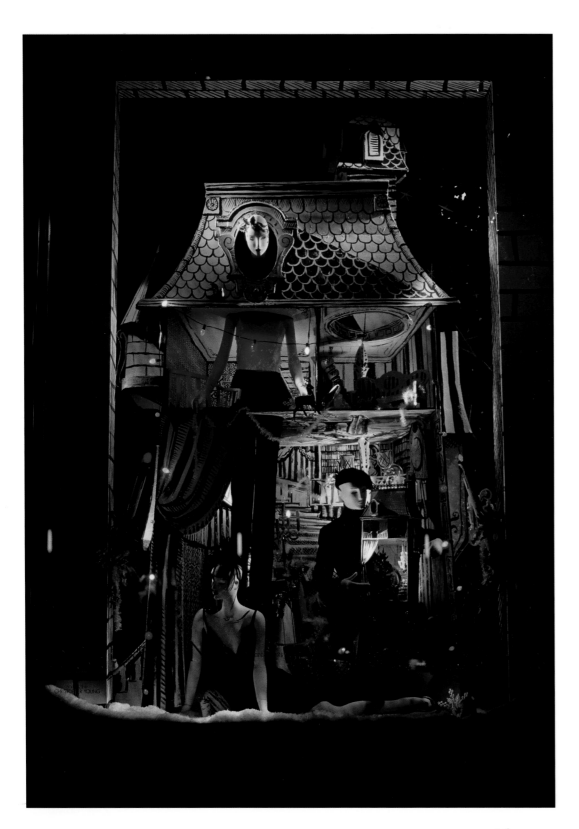

BERGDORF GOODMAN
CHRISTMAS WINDOW

Christmas and winter holiday decorations are a huge attraction of New York City; millions of tourists and residents include in their holiday schedules a stroll along Fifth Avenue that takes in the Christmas tree and skating rink at Rockefeller Center, the large toy store F.A.O. Schwarz in Trump Tower, and the many gaily-lit and decorated storefronts. Not to be missed are the windows of the great Fifth Avenue emporiums such as Bergdorf Goodman, Lord & Taylor, and Saks Fifth Avenue. These displays are so popular that viewers must often queue and wait their turn patiently in roped-off lines.

Bergdorf Goodman, which is owned and operated by the Neiman Marcus Group, caters primarily to the affluent and the fashion élite. Although it is a narrow store, it is labyrinthine and intimate, lulling patrons into lingering in its many specialized departments. The jewelry selection is regarded as one of the best in the city.

Bergdorf Goodman has always prided itself on its leadership in fashion retailing, including its innovative and artistic window displays. One of a series of "Home for the Holidays" windows, this "Doll's House" is inhabited by three mannequins, one of which has clearly outgrown her dwelling. A subliminal message perhaps? Get a bigger house so you can buy more things to put in it? It's hard to say. Reaching for high art, Bergdorf Goodman windows are often somewhat inscrutable.

RADIO CITY MUSIC HALL

This brilliant Art Deco palace came about through an unlikely collaboration between the Rockefeller family and one Samuel L. "Roxy" Rothafel, a movie theater impresario who delighted in dazzling the masses. The central entertainment facility of Rockefeller Center, Radio City Music Hall opened in 1932 to present vaudeville programs mixing jazz, ballet, comedy, symphony, opera, popular music, and acrobatics, and featuring the Rockettes, a precision chorus line of tall, beautiful women. Although the hall was always well attended, those were the days of radio; programs were broadcast across the nation and families would gather around their sets to hear the show broadcast "Live, from Radio City!"

GENERAL ELECTRIC BUILDING, ROCKEFELLER CENTER

If the many philanthropic gifts of the Rockefeller family stand for anything, they must be seen as an attempt to inject a cultural component wherever the activities of the masses intersected those of business and commerce. The concept of a commercial and entertainment center surrounding a public plaza was developed in a mid-1920s plan to provide a new home for the Metropolitan Opera. John D. Rockefeller, Jr., acquired leases on plots of land large enough to contain the opera house and additional commercial buildings, which were all to be built by their respective owners. Then came the stock market crash of 1929, followed by the Great Depression. The Metropolitan Opera pulled out of the project and Rockefeller had to go it alone if anything were to be realized from his investment. Although forced to sell stock at depression-era prices and take out a $65-million loan, Rockefeller proceeded with what was to be the largest privately funded commercial development ever undertaken.

By 1940, all the original fourteen buildings, clad in Indiana limestone with window columns providing vertical "striping," had been completed on the 17-acre site.

Over the entrance to the General Electric Building presides the statue of *Genius*, masterfully executed in Art Deco style by Lee Lawrie, with a long, flowing beard, spreading his compass above a screen composed of 240 blocks of glass.

ST. PATRICK'S CATHEDRAL

Across the street from Rockefeller Center, with its 7-ton statue of Atlas holding up the world, stands St. Patrick's, the largest Catholic cathedral in the United States. The site was originally purchased in 1828 for use as a graveyard by the two most important Catholic churches in the city, St. Peter's and the (now) Old St. Patrick's, still located on Mulberry Street, north of Little Italy. Archbishop John Hughes' announcement in 1850 that a magnificent cathedral would be built on the site instead caused some consternation: wealthy New Yorkers at that time were mostly Protestant. Although the Catholic community had since the early 1840s been bolstered by huge waves of Italian and Irish immigrants, they were mostly poor and working-class people, with hardly the resources to support a world-class cathedral.

To design the cathedral, the Archbishop turned to the native New York architect James Renwick, whose major commissions until then included Grace Church and the New York Public Library. Interestingly, although Renwick had studied engineering at Columbia University, graduating at age eighteen, he never formally studied architecture. His talent and interest in the subject derived entirely from the cultivated background he had acquired as a member of a wealthy and prominent family. But the building he designed, in the manner of the Gothic ecclesiastical architecture of Europe from the thirteenth to fifteenth centuries (for example, the cathedrals at Rheims and Cologne), is admired for its purity of style and harmony of proportions. It fulfills admirably the goal of all cathedrals: to inspire humankind to strive for the exalted state that God's plan for them promises.

SHOPPING ON FIFTH AVENUE

Saks Fifth Avenue epitomizes both the elegant shopping available on upper Fifth Avenue and the New York tradition of innovation in retailing. The store was the brainchild of Horace Saks and Bernard Gimbel, who operated independent retail stores at Herald Square at the turn of the century, and dreamed of creating an emporium for cutting-edge fashion further uptown. A site was purchased and the new store, the first large retail operation in what was then a wealthy residential neighborhood, opened in 1924. Today, Saks Fifth Avenue has 61 stores throughout 23 states, and its parent company, Saks Incorporated, operates nearly 300 more department stores under various other names.

TWENTY-ONE CLUB

The Eighteenth Amendment to the Constitution that went into effect in 1920, popularly known as Prohibition, was fairly well disliked in New York, and savvy entrepreneurs began looking for ways around the law. Thus was born the "speakeasy"—an illegal, private club selling liquor. None was more famous than Jack and Charlie's 21, founded by two cousins from the West Side, Jack Kriendler and Charlie Berns, and named after its street address. Here the rich and well-connected drank the finest wines and spirits, ate exceptionally good food, and danced to the Charleston. After Prohibition was repealed in 1933, the club "went legit," and is still considered one of the best restaurants in the city.

VILLARD HOUSES

Decked in holiday lights and seemingly out of place among the adjacent offices and shops, is this row of six handsome townhouses lining Madison Avenue between 50th and 51st Streets. The houses were built in 1882–83 by railroad tycoon Henry Villard, and were designed around this central courtyard to resemble an Italian palazzo. However, Villard went bankrupt soon after he moved into the largest of the houses, and the complex went through a number of successive owners. Nearly a century later, with the exception of the truly opulent Villard House, which occupied the south side of the courtyard, all of the sumptuous townhouses had been gutted and renovated for various office uses. The whole block was eventually purchased in 1980 by real estate developer Harry Helmsley, who planned to demolish the houses and to build a high-rise hotel on the site. Preservationists were outraged.

Facing public pressure, Helmsley wisely decided to cantilever his 51-story hotel tower partly over the townhouses and incorporate them into its lobby facilities. At a cost of about $10 million, he then meticulously renovated most of the interiors in the south wing, including a large gilded, barrel-vaulted music room with murals by John LaFarge. Prior to the completion of the project, few New Yorkers had seen the spectacular Villard interiors, which are among the finest in the city. Now that they are integrated into the New York Palace Hotel, they are preserved for all to stroll through and enjoy.

POLICE HORSE, THEATER DISTRICT

The Mounted Unit of the New York Police Department is deployed in six "troops," housed in police stables around the city. These are supported by a civilian staff, which includes hostlers and farriers. The Mounted Unit is primarily used for crowd and traffic control, at which it excels; its members are called out for concerts, outdoor entertainment events, street fairs, strikes, and demonstrations. In such situations a single mounted officer is estimated to be as effective as ten on foot.

TIMES SQUARE

In 1904 the *New York Times* produced a rooftop fireworks display to celebrate both the opening of its brand-new headquarters and its new street address, which was changed from Longacre Square to Times Square. The venerable newspaper has long since moved on, but the building at 1 Times Square is still the focus of worldwide attention when its illuminated ball drops to mark the New Year. Although the 1970s and 80s saw a Times Square in decline, a booming economy and a state-supported master plan for renovation have turned things around. Each year this premier entertainment center draws nearly 30 million tourists who spend approximately $11.6 billion.

THEATER DISTRICT

Times Square, where Seventh Avenue and Broadway intersect, is the heart of the Theater District. The expressions "on Broadway" and "the Broadway play" both derive from the name of that major thoroughfare, sometimes called "the great white way," because of the many brightly lit marquees and billboards along it. A Broadway production can be seen at a cost of between $60 and $90 in any of the nearly 40 theaters in the district, which extends from 41st to 53rd Streets. However, budget-conscious theatergoers can wait in line for a bargain at the discount ticket outlet or choose to take in a show at one of the nearly 200 off-Broadway and off-off-Broadway theaters scattered throughout the city.

TRANSFORMING TIMES SQUARE

Millions of dollars have been poured into an ambitious scheme to renovate Times Square. While most applaud the refurbished theaters and new high-rise office complexes, others are nostalgic for that which has been replaced. Architectural critic Herbert Muschamp ascribes this to the venerable urban tradition of *nostalgie de la boue*, or the sentimental attachment to decrepitude and sleaze. According to Muschamp: "After years of inertia, 42nd Street is at last well on its way to becoming a place. In effect, it's a stage-set 42nd Street. Nothing wrong with that in a theater district, so long as something culturally valuable is encouraged to take the stage."

SOLOW BUILDING, 9 WEST 57TH STREET

Walking the streets of New York City is a both a joy and an adventure, and the observant stroller will certainly encounter scenes that are both puzzling and whimsical.

Watching others registering no reaction, the visitor feels reluctant to ask the essential question: "What is it?" In this case, a helpful lobby attendant provided the answer: "No, it's not an *e*, but (when seen from the other side) a big, red *9*."

Why? Because this is 9 West 57th Street, and Sheldon Solow, the real estate developer who built the brilliant and controversial building it announces, wants everyone to know its proper address.

CARNEGIE HALL

German immigrant Leopold Damrosch founded both the Oratorio Society and the New York Symphony Society in the 1870s, but died before finding a permanent home for his fledgling organizations. His quest was carried on by his son Walter, who won the support of steel tycoon Andrew Carnegie. The Music Hall Company of New York was formed and land purchased for the construction of a new venue. To design the building, Carnegie hired the architect William B. Tuthill, who was also an excellent musician. Carnegie Hall was inaugurated with a five-day music festival in 1890, during which the composer Peter Ilyich Tchaikovsky conducted several of his works.

CARNEGIE DELI

The great delicatessens of New York were mostly started by Jewish immigrants, and feature the excellent corned beef and pastrami recipes developed in Eastern Europe. Carnegie Deli, on Seventh Avenue between 54th and 55th Streets and named after the famous music hall nearby, is the place to go if you are really hungry and honestly are not counting calories. It is an emporium of delightful delicacies, with whimsical names such as "Fifty Ways to Love Your Liver" and "Hamalot." Try a "Pistol" (deli slang for a pastrami sandwich), or, if you are quite ravenous, a "Carnegie Haul," a triple-decker sandwich with pastrami, tongue, and salami.

NEW YORK—AN INTERNATIONAL CENTER FOR DANCE

New York City has always been a center for the performing arts, including dance—the first documented dance performance dates to 1739. By the end of the eighteenth century, the city was part of a tour circuit for cultural performances that included Boston, Philadelphia, and Charleston. In the nineteenth century, dance performances included classical ballet, pantomime, Irish clogging, and black minstrel shows. By the end of the century, modern dance was being developed by Isadora Duncan and others. In 1909 an American school of ballet was established by the Metropolitan Opera, and by the 1930s the city had become the center for dance in the world.

BROADWAY DANCE CENTER

Richard Ellner, who founded the Broadway Dance Center in 1984, accurately foresaw the demand of the performing arts community for a single studio that addressed the needs of all dancers. It was a benchmark in the development of dance education to offer a diversified selection of classes, representing all dance disciplines and levels. Today the Center, which has excellent programs, facilities, and faculty, attracts students from all over the world; 5000 each month attend classes in ballet, tap, jazz, hip hop-funk, and modern dance.

This venerable midtown establishment was first opened in 1926 by former members of the Russian Imperial Ballet. After 1933, when Prohibition ended, it evolved from a sedate tearoom into a watering-hole noted for its élite clientele, elegant cuisine, and international flavor. For decades it was renowned as "Hollywood East."

Long-time owner Sidney Kaye was primarily responsible for the success of what might have been just another bar. The Russian Tea Room reflected his idiosyncratic tastes, which included the display of Christmas decorations throughout the entire year. Thus when the tearoom was sold to Warner LeRoy in 1995, patrons worried that its glory days were over. If anything, however, extensive renovations produced an establishment more exotic than ever.

A Broadway producer and director as well as a craftsman and designer, LeRoy had already applied his flair for the dramatic to several restaurant ventures, including Maxwell's Plum, for two decades perhaps the most popular restaurant in the city. To the new tearoom he brought the 500-square-foot glass ceiling, made up of 250,000 pieces of Tiffany glass, which he had created for Maxwell's Plum. He also commissioned a 15-foot aquarium in the shape of a dancing bear. Weighing over a ton, the bear is filled with live clown fish. We can only presume that they enjoy watching the patrons of this very popular tourist attraction.

NEW YORK STATE THEATER, LINCOLN CENTER

The New York State Theater opened in 1964, shortly after the inauguration in 1962 of the first building in the new Lincoln Center for the Performing Arts, Philharmonic Hall, since renamed Avery Fisher Hall. Designed by Philip Johnson and Richard Foster, the New York State Theater is home to both the New York City Ballet and the New York City Opera. Other important constituents of Lincoln Center include the Metropolitan Opera House, the Juilliard School of Music, the New York Public Library for the Performing Arts, the Mitzi E. Newhouse and Walter Reade Theaters, the Vivian Beaumont Theater, and the Alice Tully Hall, which together attract more than five million visitors each year.

METROPOLITAN OPERA HOUSE, LINCOLN CENTER

"The Met", as it is fondly called by its many fans and supporters, is one of the world's leading opera companies. Formed in 1883, the Metropolitan Opera Company first made its home at Broadway and 39th Street, in a 3700-seat hall built by a group of wealthy businessmen who couldn't get boxes at the more prestigious Academy of Music on 14th Street (which eventually went out of business). Although it was clear almost from the beginning that the new opera house lacked adequate stage facilities, it would be nearly eight decades before the Met eventually found a new home at the Lincoln Center for the Performing Arts. This new Metropolitan Opera House, designed by Wallace K. Harrison, opened in 1966 and boasts the finest technical facilities.

Met patrons have always enjoyed great stars—Enrico Caruso performed there more times than with any other company—and great conductors—for two seasons both Arturo Toscanini and Gustav Mahler were on the roster. The company has given the American premières of some of the most important works in its repertory, including *Boris Godunov*, *Turandot*, and several Wagnerian masterpieces, and has presented 29 world premières. On Christmas Day of 1931, *Hansel und Gretel* became the first opera of the Met's regular live radio broadcasts, and in 1977, a performance of *La Bohème*, viewed by more than four million people, initiated a regular series of televised productions. Each season the Metropolitan stages more than 200 performances of opera in New York, attended by more than 800,000 people.

LINCOLN CENTER FOR THE PERFORMING ARTS

The largest and most famous performing arts center in the United States, Lincoln Center was conceived in the mid-1950s, when a number of venerable New York institutions, including the New York Philharmonic and the Metropolitan Opera, were in search of better facilities. A west-side slum between 62nd and 66th Streets was approved for urban renewal, two Rockefellers (John D., Jr., and John D., III) provided financial backing, and President Dwight D. Eisenhower broke ground for construction in 1959. Aside from its outstanding resident companies, Lincoln Center has become well-known for its innovative programs, including the Mostly Mozart festival and Classical Jazz series.

MANHATTAN AT DAWN

"I want to wake up in a city, that doesn't sleep," sang Frank Sinatra in the song *New York, New York*. Francis Albert Sinatra, America's premier romantic balladeer, was born in 1915 in a tough, working-class neighborhood of Hoboken, New Jersey, just across the river from New York City. When Sinatra died in 1998, city council speaker Peter Vallone introduced legislation that would make Sinatra's recording the city's official song. Although that never came about, the song remains the quintessential expression of the aspirations of those who come to make it big in the big city: "If I can make it there, I'll make it anywhere. It's up to you—New York, New York."

MAIN READING ROOM, NEW YORK PUBLIC LIBRARY

It is surprising to note that the New York Public Library, used annually by more than ten million people, has been in existence a mere century. Funds bequeathed by New York Governor Samuel J. Tilden, to "establish and maintain a free library and reading room in the city of New York," were used in 1895 to join the two great existing New York libraries of the day, the Astor Library and the Lenox Library. While these had been bequests to the public, admission and hours were restricted, and by the 1890s, both were in financial difficulty. The monumental Beaux Arts building, designed by Carrère & Hastings to house the joint collection, opened in 1911.

PORTRAIT OF A BUILDING

What is a successful businessman to do when he has all the money he could possibly want? In New York of the 1920s and 30s, the answer might well be to build the world's tallest building. The problem was that others were doing the same thing, so while the latest "world's tallest building" was being completed in 1929—the 927-foot Bank of Manhattan at 40 Wall Street—auto magnate Walter Chrysler kept his plan to top it a secret. As his construction team worked on architect William van Alen's plans for a 925-foot building at 42nd Street and Lexington Avenue, permits were quietly secured for a 123-foot spire of stainless steel to crown it. The tower, constructed by steelworkers inside the building to keep it from public view, was then pushed through a hole in the roof to reach 1048 feet, making the 77-story Chrysler Building not only the tallest building in the world, but the tallest structure as well, topping the then record-holding Eiffel Tower.

Although that new record was to stand only briefly—the Empire State Building was completed the following year—the slender, soaring Chrysler Building is considered one of the city's most impressive and recognizable skyscrapers.

The details of the Chrysler Building are at once elegant and whimsical. Its lobby, finished in fine African woods and marbles, is an Art Deco treasure. Each of its 32 high-speed elevators features wood inlays from different parts of the world. *The World Atlas of Architecture* sings its praises: "Art Deco in France found its American equivalent in the design of the New York skyscrapers of the 1920s. The Chrysler Building…was one of the most accomplished essays in the style." As might be expected, the Chrysler Corporation's promotional booklet for its new headquarters was also breathlessly laudatory: "Into the empyrean, the builder has flung his handiwork seeking to pierce the ever-unfathomable bove"

profile and luxurious appointments wever, the building's massive quantities of steel trumpet its automotive heritage. Its gargoyles are nothing more than overgrown hood ornaments and the designs of the decorative spire bricks are taken from hubcaps. A more balanced appraisal comes only with the passage of time, in this case, a half-century, when Paul Goldberger wrote in *The City Observed* that: "The quality of the Chrysler comes from its ability to be romantic and irrational, and yet not quite so foolish as to be laughable; it stops just short, and therefore retains a shred of credibility amid the fantasy—rather like New York itself."

Above the old downtown area, the streets of Manhattan are laid out in an easy-to-follow grid pattern. Avenues running the length of the island are intersected at right angles by numbered streets running across them. The one glaring exception is Broadway, which slices from northwest to southeast along the route of an old Native American trail and so was a well-traveled thoroughfare long before the grid pattern was developed. Odd angles are thus formed wherever Broadway intersects a main avenue. (Times Square, Herald Square, and Union Square are three such irregular plots, although why they are called squares rather than triangles is a mystery.)

Here at Broadway and Fifth Avenue, a slim, pie-shaped piece of land is home to the striking Flatiron Building. Originally named the Fuller Building, after its developer, it soon succumbed to the obvious title that its shape inspired.

There are "Flatiron Buildings" in several cities, but New York's is special. At 300 feet, it was the world's tallest building when completed in 1902. And its dramatic shape, designed to take advantage of its odd site, quickly won it many admirers. Among them was the writer H.G. Wells, who likened the sharp northern edge of the building to the prow of a ship coursing through the traffic of Broadway.

To attain its record height of 300 feet in 1902, the Flatiron Building employed a steel frame, and thus it heralded the golden era of skyscrapers in New York City. The architectural firm commissioned was headed by Daniel H. Burnham, who with his partner, John Wellborn Root, had pioneered the use of steel-frame skyscraper construction in Chicago. Although a modernist when it came to construction techniques, Burnham wisely chose to soften the stark shape imposed by the narrow triangular plot with ornate French Renaissance details worked in stone and terracotta. Also notable are the three eight-story window bays that lend a soft undulation to what might otherwise be a dizzyingly sheer wall of limestone. The building's decoration is an excellent example of the "Academic Eclecticism" that Burnham became famous for.

Born in Henderson, New York, in 1846, Daniel Burnham was one of America's greatest architects. His other commissions included several landmark buildings in Chicago, as well as Union Station in Washington, D.C. (1909), Filene's Store in Boston (1912), and Selfridge's Store in London (1909). But he was most famous as a city planner; his plan for Chicago, which included huge tracts of unspoiled forest ringing the city, anticipated environmental concerns of a half-century later and was prepared long before such comprehensive urban planning was even recognized as an important and useful activity. He ultimately prepared plans for several cities, including Cleveland, San Francisco, and Baltimore, and in 1905, at the request of the United States government, he drew up plans for cities in the Philippines, including Manila.

CIRCLE LINE PIER

To really appreciate Manhattan as an island and New York's history as a great port, one must get out from under the shadows of skyscrapers and down on the water to see some of the city's 578 miles of waterfront. The Circle Line, dubbed "America's Favorite Boat Ride," has been catering to this urge for over 50 years. It offers a variety of excursions, but the most exciting and educational is the full three-hour, 35-mile cruise around Manhattan—up the East River, through the Harlem River separating Manhattan from the mainland, down the Hudson River on the West Side, and, of course, under many of the city's great bridges.

NEW YORK HARBOR

The interpretation of America's Statue of Liberty as a beacon of freedom for the world's oppressed was strengthened by the refugee experience. Most would spend several days in immigration processing on Ellis Island (middle left). Across the water, Lady Liberty beckoned all who entered New York Harbor to the golden promise of America. These thoughts were eloquently expressed by Emma Lazarus in an 1883 sonnet, "The New Colossus," in which the statue speaks: "Give me your tired, your poor / Your huddled masses yearning to breathe free / The wretched refuse of your teeming shore / Send these, the homeless, tempest-tost to me / I lift my lamp beside the golden door!"

Two of the most popular beliefs about the Statue of Liberty are that it was given to the United States by the French government and that it was intended as a beacon of hope for refugees around the globe. In fact, constructing the monument was a joint effort between the ordinary citizens of France, who were to design and build the statue, and the American people, who were to raise funds for the base. Its purpose was to reaffirm the friendship between the two countries—France had been instrumental in helping the colonies win their independence from England—and to commemorate the 100th anniversary, in 1876, of the American Revolution. On the tablet held by "Lady Liberty" is July 4, 1776, the date of the American Declaration of Independence.

But things did not go very smoothly at first. Although funds were raised by every means possible, including lotteries and prize fights, they were slow in coming. The famous newspaperman Joseph Pulitzer was so exasperated at the pace of donations, he used the editorial pages of his newspaper, *The World*, to criticize the wealthy for their stinginess, and the middle class for assuming the rich would do everything for them. Shamed into contributing, the public finally came through with the needed funds. In 1885 the statue was shipped to New York, where it was placed on its pedestal the following year, ten years behind schedule, but agreed by all to have been worth the effort.

Designed by sculptor Frédéric Auguste Bartholdi, "Lady Liberty" is one of the most widely recognized structures in the world. Interestingly, when the sculptor needed an engineer to assist him with this massive project, he turned for help to the designer of another well-known monument—Alexandre Gustave Eiffel. Together, they devised a system to attach 31 tons of copper sheathing for the statue's "skin" over 125 tons of steel structural members. The statue was then broken down into 350 individual pieces and shipped to the United States on the French frigate *Isere*.

It was reassembled in four months and set on a new granite pedestal installed inside the courtyard of the star-shaped walls of Fort Wood, which had been built for the War of 1812. "We will not forget that Liberty has here made her home; nor shall her chosen altar be neglected," said President Grover Cleveland as he accepted the Statue of Liberty on behalf of the United States in 1886.

Boats take visitors from the ferry station at the foot of Battery Park to Liberty Island, where they can climb the 192 steps to the observation platform on the pedestal or the 354 steps (22 stories) to the crown. It is a popular destination—a visit to the crown can often mean a two- to three-hour wait in line. For the less ambitious, there is a museum located in the pedestal's base where one can view exhibits on the monument's conception, construction, and restoration in 1986.

From the ground to the tip of the torch, which today is closed to visitors, the statue is 305 feet high.

ELLIS ISLAND

John F. Kennedy wrote: "There were probably as many reasons for coming to America as there were people who came." And come they did. Named after a merchant who purchased it in the eighteenth century and later sold it to the government, Ellis Island was the headquarters of the local office of the Immigration and Naturalization Service from 1892 to 1954. During that time about twelve million immigrants entered the country through it. Closed in 1954, the immigration station was dedicated as a museum in 1990. Ellis Island stands as a reminder that the United States is a nation of immigrants, and that the surest path to greatness is through offering opportunity to all.

A SYMBOL OF FREEDOM

According to the study *Lady Liberty, the Changing Face of Freedom* (available on the website of the University of Virginia), images of America's favorite icon hark back to the country's European discovery, when the untamed New World was symbolized first as a voluptuous but stern "Indian Queen," and later a tawny, barefoot, sweet-natured "Indian Princess." Those images were ultimately melded with emblems of the Greek goddess popularized by European schools of classical art and architecture. The Greek goddess represented what the eager new country of the United States aspired to: the order and sovereignty of an ancient democratic state.

ISLE OF HOPE

For immigrants arriving at Ellis Island the dream of America must have seemed so near yet so far. Their ship docked first at what are now the Chelsea Piers in Manhattan, where first- and second-class passengers debarked, having previously undergone a courteously administered on-board inspection. Only steerage passengers were then taken to Ellis Island, where they were subject to a battery of medical exams and questions, typically administered with the aid of interpreters. Although cursory by today's standards, the tests were a source of incredible anxiety; a doctor marking you with white chalk meant you would be detained for further examination, and if you failed you would be deported.

GOVERNORS ISLAND

Situated between Brooklyn and the Statue of Liberty, this 173-acre island occupies a strategic spot at the entrance to New York Harbor. In 1794 Fort Jay was established on a high point on the island, and in the early 1800s gun batteries were built on the northern and southern ends. When in 1996 the federal government decided the island no longer had any military value, it offered to sell it to New York and New Jersey for $1 each, a good price for a prime piece of real estate with Manhattan skyline views. Suggestions for development include low-cost housing, public parkland, a sports complex, an education center, and conference facilities for the United Nations.

CHESS PLAYERS, WASHINGTON SQUARE

In 1857 chess legend Paul Morphy won the first national tournament held in the United States, in New York City, and went on to defeat the world's best players of the day. Although Morphy was from New Orleans, his astounding exploits (in Paris, he defeated six players while blindfolded) were chiefly responsible for popularizing chess in the city. In the early twentieth century, chess tournaments were organized and dominated by chess clubs. The two most influential were the Manhattan Chess Club and the Marshall Chess Club on West 10th Street. A meet between the two clubs was a highlight of the annual competition schedule.

STREET PERFORMER, WASHINGTON SQUARE

The dream of New York City, the stage where all who aspire to "make it big" must perform, was perhaps best expressed by American writer E.B. White: "...whether it is the farmer arriving from Italy to set up a small grocery store in a slum, or a young girl arriving from Mississippi to escape the indignity of being observed by her neighbors, or a boy arriving from the Corn Belt with a manuscript in his suitcase and a pain in his heart, it makes no difference: each embraces New York with the intense excitement of a first love, each absorbs New York with the fresh eyes of an adventurer, each generates heat and light to dwarf the Consolidated Edison Company."

WASHINGTON SQUARE

Construction of the stone arch at Washington Square in the 1890s led to the literal unearthing of a long-buried secret, when every shovelful of earth brought up human bones. It turned out that the park had formerly been the site of several graveyards, including a "potter's field" used to bury the nameless dead, as well as miscreants who had been hung at the public gallows there. The potter's field was closed in 1826, and by the turn of the next century, Greenwich Village was a picturesque village embedded in a city that had grown all around it. It still boasts enough crooked, winding, narrow streets to allow visitors to conjure images of the nineteenth-century city.

WASHINGTON SQUARE ARCH

Standing where Fifth Avenue ends at Washington Square Park, this stone arch replaces one made of wood that was erected on the same spot on April 30, 1889, to honor the 100th anniversary of the inauguration of George Washington. People were so thrilled with the design of Stanford White, based on the triumphal arches of Roman times, that the architect was commissioned to build a permanent version. The arch has become the most notable landmark in Greenwich Village and its unofficial entrance, while the park is the stage for a variety of street performers. Students, tourists, dog walkers, chess players, snack vendors, lovers, and police fill the park on a bright spring day.

CHRISTOPHER PARK, GREENWICH VILLAGE

The installation of George Segal's statues of two gay couples in the 1990s provoked no more controversy than normal for the residents of Christopher Street, which in recent decades has been the center of gay life in the city. It was on this street that the Stonewall Rebellion of 1969 launched the gay rights movement. The intellectual power and creative energy of New York City's gay community has been the nation's greatest weapon in the fight against AIDS. Where Christopher Street joins Waverly stands the Northern Dispensary, the city's oldest medical clinic, established in 1827 to provide medical care for the poor. It has now been converted into a residence for homeless people with AIDS.

STONEWALL PLACE

Many tourists mistake this tiny park for nearby Sheridan Square, as it contains a statue of Philip Sheridan, a noted Union general during the Civil War, who later commanded troops in the western states. Behind the park is the Stonewall Inn, a popular gay club that in June of 1969 was raided by police, igniting what is now called the Stonewall Rebellion. Gay residents poured into the street in protest, leading to several nights of civil disobedience and numerous arrests. In commemoration, this part of Christopher Street is now called Stonewall Place.

GREENWICH VILLAGER, THOMPSON STREET

Strolling through Greenwich Village one encounters all kinds of characters, most of whom gravitate here because it seems more suited to their individualism than do other parts of the city. The Village has always been home to the odd, the idiosyncratic, the creative. Walk in any direction and you pass a landmark associated with some famous writer. Edna St. Vincent Millay or John dos Passos could have been spotted at the Brevoort Hotel on 8th Street; Willa Cather and Theodore Dreiser wrote novels nearby; and Norman Mailer and Dylan Thomas both drank at the White Horse Tavern on Hudson Street.

CIGAR-STORE INDIAN

The tobacco plant is native to the Americas; thus its association with Native Americans is not surprising. Smoking some sort of dried weed was a practice in Mayan culture more than a thousand years ago and there are several documented encounters between the smokers of the New World and the first European explorers there.

During his 1492 voyage, Christopher Columbus met "Indian" smokers in the Caribbean, and both he and the Spanish conquistador Hernando Cortes took tobacco seeds back to Europe. By the end of the sixteenth century, tobacco had become a valuable commodity in global trade.

The origin of the wooden "Indian" dates back to those early days of importing tobacco into England, when tobacco companies were recognized by the display of small wooden figures called "Virginie Men." The statues got their name from a group of Native Americans who were known to live around the first permanent English settlement in America, at Jamestown, Virginia. Still, depicted as black men wearing headdresses and kilts made of tobacco leaves, they looked nothing like real Native Americans. This form of signage soon proliferated in America as well, but the figures were blown up to life-size and began to be imbued with more realistic detail. Colorful headdresses and fringed buckskins, and sometimes holding tomahawks or spears, cigar-store Indians grabbed the attention of passers-by, many of them immigrants who could not read the English words "Tobacconist Shop."

Today, vintage cigar-store Indians are highly valued by collectors.

PLAYERS THEATRE AND CAFE WHA?, GREENWICH VILLAGE

In 1915 the playwright Eugene O'Neill arrived in Greenwich Village, settled down at 38 Washington Square, and began writing plays. His dark vision and gritty realism were to change American theater. As one reviewer put it: "Before O'Neill, the United States had theater; after O'Neill, it had drama." O'Neill was instrumental in establishing the Provincetown Players in Greenwich Village—in MacDougal Street just up from the present Players Theatre—where the company staged premiers of many of his works. O'Neill went on to win two Pulitzer Prizes (for *Beyond the Horizon* and *Anna Christie*) as well as the Nobel Prize for Literature.

O'Neill was succeeded as the major innovator in American theater by Edward Albee, who arrived in the late 1940s and lived in a variety of cheap apartments in Greenwich Village and nearby Little Italy. Although Albee's greatest commercial success was *Who's Afraid of Virginia Woolf?*, his first play, *The Zoo Story*, was written in his West 4th Street apartment and first staged by O'Neill's Provincetown Players.

The Players Theatre shown here was established in 1952, in a building that formerly was a stable. Another Village standby is the Cafe Wha? next door, a nightspot featuring classic rock and roll, rhythm and blues, and reggae. MacDougal and Bleecker Streets still vibrate with the creative energy that has always been a Village hallmark.

VILLAGE LIFE

Early in the twentieth century, "the Village" was well-known for its bohemian population. During that time it acquired a reputation as a place for avant-garde thinking, both political and artistic, which it maintains today. New York University was established on the east side of the park, many galleries, literary salons, and libraries moved in, and artists and writers found it a congenial place for their creative activities. Radical and non-conformist ideas and movements are a Village tradition, and include the "beat movement" of the 1950s, the antiwar movement of the 1960s and 70s, and the gay liberation movement of the 1980s.

GARMENT WORKERS' PROTEST

New York City has always been the center of organized labor activity in the United States, and most of the powerful national labor organizations had their origins here in the nineteenth century. It was not always a congenial environment—early strikes were often prosecuted as conspiracies, and 1850 saw the first American worker (a tailor) killed in a trade dispute. But the labor movement slowly gained ground. Strikes in the 1880s won many workers eight-hour workdays for the first time. New York City is still more unionized than the rest of the nation. Here, a protest against illegal sweatshops begins in front of the Woolworth Building, just below City Hall.

NEW YORK'S FINEST

As the city's population swelled to over half a million people by the mid-nineteenth century, a municipal police force was formed to deal with the urban problems of slums, crime, and rioting. However, with police officers beholden for two years to the politicians who had appointed them, the new system proved corrupt and unworkable. Reform and efficiency were finally instituted by an iron-willed new head of the police board, Theodore Roosevelt, later to become the 26th President of the United States. Today, the New York Police Department has 39,000 uniformed officers of all ranks, supported by approximately 9000 civilians, and an annual budget of $2.4 billion.

VESUVIO BAKERY, SOHO

New York City's association with Italy is old and strong; the harbor was first explored by an Italian, Giovanni da Verrazano, in 1524. But Italians did not begin to make up a major part of the population until the early twentieth century, when from 1899 to 1910 nearly two million immigrants from southern Italy—mostly *contadini*, or landless farmers—poured into the country, perhaps a quarter of them settling in New York City. Men typically worked in the construction trades, women in the garment industry. There were many "Little Italys" then, in East Harlem, Williamsburg, and Greenpoint, as well as in Lower Manhattan; new arrivals tended to settle where others from their home town or province were living.

Lower Manhattan's Little Italy is today only a tourist-supported shell of what it once was; in the 1920s it spread south to Canal Street and west to Greenwich Village, which itself had a large Italian population. This well-known neighborhood bakery at 160 Prince Street, operated by Anthony Dapolito, was established by his immigrant father in 1920.

STREET MURAL, SOHO

The first art galleries in New York City were situated in Midtown, in the center of wealthy New York and close to the Museum of Modern Art on 53rd Street. The opening by Paula Cooper of a gallery on Wooster Street in 1969 reflected a shift of the center of the New York art world to SoHo (short for South of Houston Street). The high ceilings and cheap rents of this former light-industrial area were ideal for both artists and exhibitors alike. Although rising rents and gentrification soon pushed many working artists to outlying neighborhoods, SoHo is still the place to see what is happening in the New York art world, both in its numerous galleries and on its cobbled streets.

MERCER STREET,
CAST-IRON HISTORIC DISTRICT

What appears to be an intricate ornamental stone façade is, in fact, cast-iron, which has several important advantages as a building material. It is lighter than stone and does not require intense labor to embellish it with design—decorative details are simply incorporated into the molds as part of the casting process. Although the technology for producing cast-iron cheaply was a British invention, American architects were quick to make use of it, and this section of SoHo has many elegant buildings boasting cast-iron columns, lintels, arches, and cornices. Most were constructed during the second half of the nineteenth century. Neglected and run-down for decades thereafter, in the 1960s and 70s SoHo began attracting artists seeking large spaces with low rents. They were quickly followed by chic restaurants and fancy boutiques, as SoHo became the hip destination for shopping and strolling it is today.

STREET SINGER, 34TH STREET SUBWAY STATION

With more than 244 miles of routes, New York City's subway system is the most extensive in the world. It is also fairly old—the first segment opened in 1904—and consequently rather cramped and poorly ventilated. The Metropolitan Transit Authority has created several innovative programs, one of which is Arts for Transit. This program has commissioned numerous artworks—more than 60 in place and another 50 planned—for display throughout the system, leading the *New York Times* to write: "The biggest art gallery in New York is one that thousands of people pass through every day." Also part of the program is Music Under New York, which supports performances at selected stations.

KOREAN BARBECUE RESTAURANT

Korean immigration to New York in significant numbers is a fairly recent event; in 1920 there were only 70 Koreans in the city. Due to Cold War politics and immigration laws, post-1950s arrivals tended to be educated professionals, who fairly quickly enjoyed economic success and moved to the suburbs. Others used their latent entrepreneurial skills to open small businesses. This "Korea Town" strip of restaurants and shops, just south of the Empire State Building, actively supports the Korean wholesale businesses along Broadway between 23rd and 31st Streets. Favorite eateries are these "Korean barbecues," where beef and vegetables are cooked by patrons at their own table grills.

New York boasts the largest South Asian population of any American city, with Indians dominating a group that includes Pakistanis, Bangladeshis, Sri Lankans, and Nepalese. The first Indians to come to New York visited as colonial traders. Immigrants from India began arriving between the turn of the century and 1917, when court rulings barred immigrants from Asian countries. These early arrivals included political refugees, professionals, and businessmen, as well Punjabi agricultural workers who came eastward after crop failures in California.

After 1946 Indians could again become citizens, and by the 1970s, about 20,000 South Asians a year began arriving in the United States. Those who were not professionals found work as taxi drivers, autoworkers, cashiers, newsstand operators, and toll takers. Businessmen opened travel and insurance agencies, groceries, and, of course, restaurants. The Little India section of mid-Manhattan, centered on 28th Street and Lexington Avenue, boasts many of these establishments, which are favored by the city's Indian taxi drivers. Indians began settling here along Lexington Avenue after many years of shopping for spices and foodstuffs at a shop run by an Armenian named Kalustyan, a shop which is still a mainstay of the community.

STREIT'S MATZOS

Aron Streit and his wife Nettie left Europe for America in the 1890s. In 1916, Aron opened his first matzo factory on the Lower East Side, where he baked the unleavened bread eaten by Jews during Passover. In 1925, Aron and one of his sons opened a modern bakery on Rivington Street; a few years later, his other son joined the business. With the family working together, the Streit matzo bakery prospered and grew. At the matzo bakery and at home, Old World traditions, including Friday night Shabbos dinners, were maintained. Aron's great-grandchildren continue the family traditions, lighting Shabbos candles and teaching the fifth generation how to maintain Jewish values in America.

DIPALO'S FINE FOODS, LITTLE ITALY

Lower Manhattan began attracting Italian immigrants in the 1850s, and by the 1920s, Little Italy extended from Greenwich Village eastward to the Bowery. Although much diminished since then, as its residents became prosperous and moved elsewhere, the neighborhood still abounds with Italian restaurants, food shops, and bakeries. Marie, Luigi, and Salvatore now run DiPalo's Fine Foods, a fixture of Little Italy started by their grandmother in 1910. Shopping here inevitably requires a few delightful rounds of tasting and chatting to make sure you take home just the right Parmesan or prosciutto. "The counters were deliberately built low," says Marie, "so that it would feel like being at home."

FISH MARKET, CHINATOWN

In the mid-nineteenth century, Chinese immigrants began arriving in the United States in significant numbers, mostly on the west coast, attracted by the lure of the Gold Rush of 1849. San Francisco is still called in Chinese *Jiu Jin Shan*, or "Old Gold Mountain." Most who came never saw any gold, but joined other Chinese brought in by labor brokers to build the transcontinental railroad, which was completed in 1869. The majority of these migrant laborers wanted simply to make a bit of cash and return home, but others stayed on, beckoned by perceived opportunities to strike it rich. But life was hard, and the willingness of the Chinese to work long hours for lower wages made them unpopular among their fellow workers. Race prejudice drove many to the cities, where they engaged in menial work in hand laundries and "chop suey" restaurants or opened stores in Chinese areas.

Here at a Chinatown fish market, New Yorkers can enjoy part of the Chinese legacy in America. Most of the Chinese who came to the United States in the past were not well-educated Mandarins from the northern cities, but rather farmers and seafarers from the southern provinces, especially Guangzhou (formerly Canton). The cuisine of this area is prized for its use of the freshest ingredients, especially fish.

VEGETABLE MARKET, CHINATOWN

Cantonese cuisine predominantly employs the stir-fry technique, in which chopped or sliced vegetables, meat, fish, or noodles are cooked in an oiled wok with seasonings such as garlic, ginger, soy sauce, and rice wine. Because the stir-frying is done very quickly over high heat, only the freshest ingredients can be used, and Chinatown residents shop daily for the best meats and produce. Although heavily Cantonese, Chinatown's population includes immigrants from all regions of China, and nowhere else in the West can you choose from so many different styles of Chinese cuisine, from traditional Cantonese *dim sum*, to Peking Duck, Shanghai seafood, and even Buddhist vegetarian fare.

In the several square miles of New York City north and south of Canal Street and east of Broadway, lives the largest concentration of Chinese in the western hemisphere, surpassing in population even San Francisco's famed Chinatown.

The earliest Chinese to come to New York were merchants or sailors engaged in trade between the two countries, and Chinese have lived in the city since the nineteenth century. According to *The Encyclopedia of New York City* the first grocery in the neighborhood was probably the Wo Kee store, opened here on Mott Street in 1872. In spite of the growth of Chinatown in recent decades, Mott Street remains its heart.

Tourism is a mainstay of the modern Chinatown economy, and busloads of visitors from all over the world can be seen strolling through the curio shops of Mott Street and eating in some of the best Chinese restaurants in the city.

FRUIT VENDOR, CHINATOWN

During World War II, the Chinese Exclusion Act was lifted, and further changes in immigration laws in the 1960s allowed 20,000 Chinese to enter the country every year. This led to explosive growth in New York City's Chinatown, which expanded into and around Little Italy to the north. Wealthy Chinese investors bought whole downtown buildings with cash, and opened garment or light-industrial factories, with ground-floor stores and restaurants. In spite of the fact that these buildings are mostly nineteenth-century tenement buildings, space remains precious, and Chinatown rents rank with the highest in the city. Thus the solution for many entrepreneurs is the time-honored street stand.

CANAL STREET

Here, along Canal Street, one can get an impression of the wealth of Chinatown. The streets are lined with shops selling gold and diamond jewelry, as well as branches of major banks and financial institutions that deem it prudent to serve their Chinese customers in their own language. In spite of their industriousness and thrift, more likely because of it, Chinese have been the only nationality targeted (except in wartime) by an act specifically written to prevent their entry, the Chinese Exclusion Act of 1882. With the lifting of that law in 1943, the population of Chinatown has swelled to perhaps 175,000, now including Burmese, Vietnamese, Malaysians, and Filipinos.

GRAMERCY PARK

Gramercy Park is New York's only private residential square. The area was developed in 1831 by Samuel B. Ruggles from what was a 20-acre farm with a swamp where the park is now sited. Ruggles was a small-scale urban developer who reasoned that restricting access to the park to residents of the surrounding lots would enhance their value. The townhouses around Gramercy Park are now some of the finest in Manhattan, and the building at 129 East 17th Street, dating from 1879, is believed to be the oldest surviving apartment house in the city. Noteworthy also are the clubhouses on the south side of the park, including the National Arts Club.

MANHATTAN SKYLINE AT NIGHT

New York has always been known for its nightlife. One explanation for the origin of the name Manhattan is that it derives from the old Indian word *manahactanienk*, meaning "place of general inebriation." Peter Stuyvesant, governor of the new Dutch colony, complained in 1648 that a quarter of the city's houses were taverns, and proceeded to pass laws regulating their hours of business. But nightlife isn't all about drinks; those tourists who fill the city's nearly 70,000 hotel rooms (at an average of $237 per night) may just want a bite to eat (at one of 18,000 restaurants), or to see one of the 1237 different performances at the city's 162 performance spaces.

SUNRISE OVER MANHATTAN

"And the sky went wan, and the wind came cold, / And the sun rose dripping, a bucketful of gold," wrote Edna St. Vincent Millay in her poem "Recuerdo." Millay arrived in New York City in 1917, and instantly captured the heart of critic Edmund Wilson, who wrote that the poetess, when "excited by the blood or the spirit, became almost supernaturally beautiful." It was Wilson who brought her to the attention of the editors of *Vanity Fair* magazine, which then began publishing her poems. Millay, who won the Pulitzer Prize in 1923, was perhaps foremost in a group of Greenwich Village poets that included Marianne Moore, Hart Crane, and e.e. cummings.

QUEENSBORO BRIDGE

The third to be built of the eight bridges that would eventually span the East River, the Queensboro Bridge was completed in 1910. It is made up of two cantilevered sections joined by a center span resting on piers on Roosevelt Island, which is the destination of the aerial tramcar on the right. The other, perhaps more common name of the bridge was popularized by Simon and Garfunkel's *59th Street Bridge Song* a.k.a. *Feelin' Groovy* ("Slow down, you move too fast / You've got the make the morning last"). The bridge leads, as one might expect, from 59th Street in Manhattan to the borough of Queens, the largest of New York City's five boroughs.

LIGHTHOUSE, ROOSEVELT ISLAND

This narrow island in the East River had a rather notorious history. In 1673 Captain John Manning, the Sheriff of New York, was exiled to his home here for having surrendered New York's Fort James to the Dutch without firing a shot. The city purchased the island in 1828, naming it Welfare Island and building prisons, poorhouses, and hospitals on it. In 1842 Charles Dickens visited its asylum for the mentally ill and described its wretched conditions in his *American Notes*. Today Roosevelt Island is home to a large housing development, but retains several historic buildings, including this lighthouse, designed by James Renwick, and built in 1872 from stone quarried by island convicts.

In retrospect, the establishment of this museum was bound to be controversial. The wealthy collector and philanthropist Solomon R. Guggenheim, aided by his art adviser Hilla Rebay, sought a permanent home for their recently established Museum of Non-Objective Painting, then housed in a former automobile showroom on 54th Street.

Guggenheim's collection featured the radical forms of new art being created by such artists as Vasily Kandinsky, Paul Klee, and Piet Mondrian, and for a building to house them he commissioned the services of one of America's most brilliant, radical, and cantankerous architects, Frank Lloyd Wright. Arguments started from day one—Wright did not even want the building to be built in New York. The differences between architect and patron were never resolved; both died before the museum opened in 1959, when huge throngs gathered to be first to enter the amazing new building.

Yet, Wright's design is a marvel of functionality and common sense. Rather than wandering from hall to hall through warrens of small side rooms, then backtracking, as one does in most museums (who hasn't got lost in the Metropolitan Museum of Art or the Louvre?), visitors ride elevators to the breathtaking heights of a spiraling ramp. From there they can view the art on display while descending gradually and gracefully to the main floor below.

CENTRAL COURT, SOLOMON R. GUGGENHEIM MUSEUM

How, exactly, does one describe this amazing design? Spiro Kostof, writing in *A History of Architecture*, exclaims: "It is a continuous spatial helix, a circular ramp that expands as it coils vertiginously around an unobstructed well of space capped by a flat-ribbed glass dome." This is hard to visualize, but, more to the point, it *can* be felt. Frank Lloyd Wright sought to create a "temple of spirit," a structure resonating with the forms of nature, the perfect curves of great ocean waves and the delicate spirals of seashells. His goal, in his own words, "was to make the building and the painting an uninterrupted, beautiful symphony such as never existed in the World of Art before."

METROPOLITAN MUSEUM OF ART

Boasting more than two million objects and nearly five million visitors per year, the Metropolitan Museum of Art in New York City is the largest and most comprehensive art museum in the western hemisphere. Although the museum has collections of all arts in all cultures, its painting collection ranks with those of the great European repositories, and includes five of the 35 known Vermeers. "The Met" acquired two works by Edouard Manet in 1889, a work by Renoir as early as 1907, and was the first institution to accept a work by Henri Matisse, in 1910. The museum has one of the world's great collections of Impressionist and Post-Impressionist art.

A STOREHOUSE OF WORLD ART

The Metropolitan Museum of Art was the brainchild of several members of the Union League Club, which had been formed in 1863 with the primary purpose of supporting the Union cause in the Civil War. A site along Fifth Avenue was acquired for the museum's growing collection, which had been housed in temporary facilities for a decade, and the city raised half a million dollars through taxes to build a red-brick building in the neo-Gothic style. That older building (right) is today joined with a glass-roofed courtyard to a 1910 addition that fronts Fifth Avenue (left).

Although the first object collected—in 1870, before the museum even had a building—was a Roman sarcophagus, the museum achieved greater notice due to a fine collection of European paintings, especially Dutch and Flemish, acquired through the purchase of three private collections. The purchase in 1873 of a collection of artifacts unearthed on Cyprus established the museum's reputation as a repository of antiquities.

Today the museum is an encyclopedic storehouse of world art. Every culture from every part of the world is represented to some degree, from the earliest times to the present, and in every medium. Highlights are one of the finest collections of ancient glass and silver in the world, an Egyptian art collection acknowledged to be the best outside of Cairo, and an exceptionally comprehensive Islamic art collection. Finally, the American Wing, as one might expect, displays the most extensive collection of American painting, sculpture, and decorative arts in the world.

TEMPLE EMANU-EL

Although the first Jews arrived in New Amsterdam in 1654 aboard the ship *St. Charles*, there was not a significant Jewish population in the city until the mid-nineteenth century, when refugees escaping European anti-Semitism began arriving in large numbers. Many settled in the Lower East Side, where the first Reform congregation in New York City was founded in 1845 as a German cultural society. The congregation grew and moved out of its rented rooms, relocating several times a bit further uptown. In the late 1920s, it merged with another Reform congregation, Beth-El, and moved into this imposing Art Deco building. The largest Reform synagogue in the world, Temple Emanu-El, meaning literally "God is with us," stands at Fifth Avenue and 65th Street, on property that was formerly the site of the John Jacob Astor mansion. The first religious service was conducted in the new sanctuary in September 1929.

In addition to its devotional services, the congregation of Temple Emanu-El has always reached out to other Jewish refugees, including those fleeing the pogroms and economic hardship of czarist Russia in the early twentieth century, and those escaping the tyranny of Nazi Germany in the 1930s. Charitable activities included social and educational programs to help ease the difficult process of Americanization. Throughout the Temple's history, its members have served as preeminent exponents of liberal and active Judaism in America.

CITY HALL PARK

This lovely park to the south of City Hall is a small triangle formed by the intersection of Park Row, which in pre-Revolutionary War days was the Boston Post Road, and Broadway. It was an important crossroads, and, planted with apple trees, it served as a common for New York residents. In July of 1776 the newly drafted Declaration of Independence was read here to George Washington and his troops. The park contains a statue of Nathan Hale, the Revolutionary War hero who was captured and hung at age 21 after boldly declaring: "I only regret that I have but one life to lose for my country."

HUDSON RIVER

The Hudson River was named after the first European to explore it, Englishman Henry Hudson, as part of the European quest for a water route across the Americas to the Far East. Hudson and his crew of twenty anchored their ship, the *Half Moon*, at this very spot (where the Hudson and Harlem Rivers meet) on September 12, 1609, and the following morning began sailing upriver. Although he explored more than 150 miles of the waterway, Hudson's quest for a Northwest Passage was doomed, as was the captain himself. On a subsequent voyage his crew mutinied, putting Hudson, his son, and seven loyal sailors adrift in a small boat. They were never seen again.

GEORGE WASHINGTON BRIDGE

Opened in 1931, this elegant bridge across the Hudson River linking New York with New Jersey held the title of the world's longest suspension bridge, until its 3500-foot main span was eclipsed by that of San Francisco's Golden Gate Bridge in 1937. Declaring it to be "the most beautiful bridge in the world," the great architect Le Corbusier said: "Made of cables and steel beams, it gleams in the sky like a reversed arch. It is blessed...When your car moves up the ramp, the two towers rise so high that it brings you happiness; their structure is so pure, so resolute, so regular that here, finally, steel architecture seems to laugh."

TOMB OF ULYSSES S. GRANT

Designed by the architect John Duncan and completed in 1897, the granite and marble tomb of the eighteenth President of the United States and his wife, Julia Dent Grant, is the largest mausoleum in North America. It is maintained by the National Park Service. Coincidentally, President Grant signed the act establishing the first national park, Yellowstone, in March of 1872. Although historians rate Ulysses S. Grant as one of the country's worst presidents, he was a highly popular war hero, given much credit for winning the American Civil War and thus keeping the country united. At his death in 1885, he was mourned by millions as the greatest American general since George Washington.

ELEVATED HIGHWAY,
UPPER WEST SIDE

New York City's traffic, and what to do with it, have been a headache since the eighteenth century, when the constant stream of vehicles and their trail of wet horse manure necessitated the building of a pedestrian bridge across Broadway near Fulton Street.

The person with the greatest impact on New York City's roads, highways, and bridges was the twentieth-century figure, Robert Moses (1888–1981). Appointed in 1924 by Governor Al Smith as President of the Long Island Parks Commission, Moses built 9700 acres of parkland on Long Island, as well as the Northern State Parkway and the Southern Parkway. Throughout his career he managed to secure important appointments, including parks commissioner of New York City, member of the city's planning commission, and head of the mayor's committee on slum clearance. He often held these positions simultaneously, which gave him control over a vast array of public projects.

A master planner and builder, Moses was the chief proponent and planner of the Harlem River Drive, the Long Island Expressway, the Triborough and Verrazano Narrows bridges, numerous housing developments, two World's Fairs (1939 and 1964), as well as Shea Stadium, the United Nations, and the Lincoln Center. Although criticized today for ignoring mass transportation and thus responsible for the city's endemic gridlock, Robert Moses' legacy is indeed staggering—there is no place in the city one can turn without seeing some evidence of his life's work.

DETAIL, CATHEDRAL CHURCH OF ST. JOHN THE DIVINE

Since it began in 1892, construction of St. John the Divine has been beset by delays, mostly due to the financial constraints of building such a colossal Gothic monument in modern times. Progress was halted from the onset of World War II through the near-bankruptcy of the city in the late 1960s. It was the Very Rev. James Parks Morton, dean at the time, who pressed for a revival of the building program. But he wisely conceived it as a way to attain two of the church's major objectives: support for the needs of the community and the artistic expression of its love of God. Morton's solution was that the cathedral would hire and train the unemployed and underemployed from the neighborhood to do the work. He boldly stated: "We will revive the art of stonecraft...and provide our city with a massive symbol of hope and rebirth."

In 1979, the Stoneyard was dedicated. However, stonecraft was a moribund skill in the United States, so professionals had to be brought from England to train the stoneworkers. Finally, in 1982, the next phase of construction began.

The cathedral's many supporters and admirers can take heart in the words of then mayor Edward Koch as he addressed a gathering for the dedication of the Stoneyard. "I am told," he said, "that some of the great cathedrals took over 500 years to build. But I would like to remind you that we are only in our first 100 years."

CATHEDRAL CHURCH OF ST. JOHN THE DIVINE

The cornerstone for this Episcopalian cathedral was laid on St. John's Day, December 27, 1892. Today, more than a century later, the building is still only two-thirds finished. Fifteen years after construction began, the principal architect passed away, and the newly hired firm led by Ralph Cram pushed the design in a more Gothic direction. The nave, more than 600 feet long, was finally opened in 1941, but by then World War II had halted construction again. Work on the cathedral resumed in the late 1970s. Even in its uncompleted state, this magnificent structure is the largest Gothic church in the world.

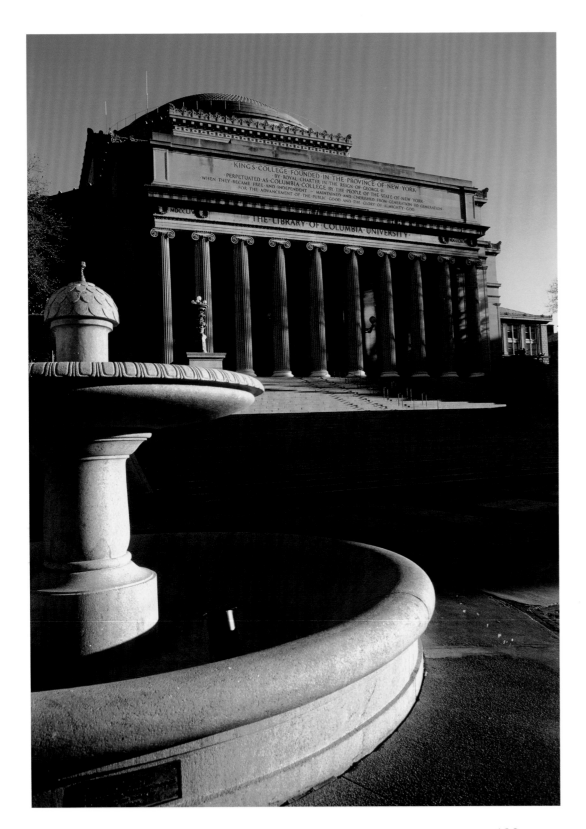

LOW MEMORIAL LIBRARY, COLUMBIA UNIVERSITY

Columbia University is the oldest institution of higher learning in the state of New York and the fifth oldest in the country. It was founded as King's College by royal charter of King George II in 1754, although, ironically, some of the great leaders of the American Revolution and the new United States of America were associated with it as students or trustees. These include Robert R. Livingston, one of the five men who drafted the Declaration of Independence; Gouverneur Morris, author of the final draft of the United States Constitution; and Alexander Hamilton, the first Secretary of the Treasury. Closed for eight years during the Revolution and its aftermath, the school reopened as Columbia College in 1784.

As Columbia grew, it moved from Park Place near City Hall to 49th Street and Madison Avenue, where it remained until it moved to its present location in Morningside Heights in 1897.

Seth Low, then president of the university and chief architect of that last move, commissioned the architectural firm of McKim, Mead & White to create an academic village in a spacious setting. The new campus, modeled after the Athenian marketplace, consequently contains the largest collection of McKim, Mead & White buildings in existence. The Low Memorial Library, named in honor of Seth Low's father, is the architectural centerpiece of the campus. Built in the Roman Classical style, it served as the main library until 1934. Today it is home to the university's central administrative offices and visitors center.

EMPIRE STATE BUILDING

Together with the Statue of Liberty, the Empire State Building, soaring majestically above the minor skyscrapers of midtown Manhattan, is one of the most recognizable symbols of New York City. Completed in 1931, the construction of what was then going to be the world's tallest building set records for speed still unsurpassed. The structure rose four and a half stories in an average week and ultimately occupied 37 million cubic feet of space over two acres. Its lobby features illuminated panels showing the traditional Seven Wonders of the World, plus an eighth: the Empire State Building.

Visitors still throng to observation platforms on the 86th and 102nd floors, where from the latter they can gaze over the city from 1250 feet. It is another 222 feet from here to the top of the tower. Although it has long since relinquished its claim as the world's tallest building, the Empire State Building remains one of the most memorable and familiar structures in the city skyline. Its distinctive, graceful outline comes to mind whenever one recalls New York. After all, this is where Charles Boyer waited for Irene Dunn in *Love Affair*, where Deborah Kerr broke Cary Grant's heart in *An Affair to Remember*, where Tom Hanks finally met Meg Ryan in *Sleepless in Seattle*, and where the beauty of Fay Wray killed the beast in *King Kong*.

ENTRANCE LOBBY, EMPIRE STATE BUILDING

The Empire State Building is hands down the world's most famous skyscraper, and well deserves admiration for its sleek and graceful form. As with any grand project, however, its history includes some quirky facts. For example, contracts for the project were signed in the fall of 1929, just a few weeks before the stock market crash that heralded the Great Depression. But construction proceeded apace, and the building was completed 45 days ahead of schedule and $5 million under budget. Spectacular as an engineering feat, however, it was not initially a financial success. Depression kept rents down and tenants few. So many offices remained empty for so long that wags were prompted to dub it the "Empty State Building."

The dome below the communication antennas was designed as a dirigible mooring. Although it never worked out successfully, due to the tricky winds at 1300 feet, it was made famous as the grip from which King Kong hung as he swatted pesky planes away.

Other activities associated with this famous structure include the Annual Empire State Building Run-Up. This race up the 1575 steps from the lobby to the 86th floor has been held every year since 1978. But if you want to participate, you had best be in shape: recent winning times have been under ten minutes.

A TRAGIC ENCOUNTER

On July 28, 1948, Lieutenant Colonel William F. Smith, Jr., a decorated veteran of 100 combat missions, was flying an unarmed B-25 bomber from Bedford, Massachusetts to Newark, New Jersey. He had planned to land at LaGuardia Airport, but because of the dense fog, Smith asked for and received permission to fly on to Newark, meaning he had to fly over Manhattan. A later investigation concluded that Smith was disoriented by the fog and assumed that he was on the west side of Manhattan, when in fact he was east of it and its tall buildings. This was to be a tragic assumption; turning south and west Smith rammed at 200 miles per hour into the 79th floor of the Empire State Building at 9:40 a.m.

The impact gouged an 18 by 20-foot hole into the building, shattering windows and sending glass flying and dropping to the street. Exploding fuel tanks sent a fireball down the corridors, and one of the plane's engines plowed through the building, emerging on the 33rd Street side and crashing through the roof of another building. Another engine and part of its landing gear fell through an elevator shaft. In all, fourteen people died, eleven in the building plus Lieutenant Colonel Smith and two passengers. If anything good can be thought of the tragedy, it is that it happened on a weekend. At the time there were only about 1500 people in the Empire State Building, compared with up to 15,000 on an average weekday.

JAMES A. FARLEY
GENERAL POST OFFICE

On a rainy Monday morning in 1963, workers commenced tearing down one of the greatest masterpieces of New York City architecture, the old Pennsylvania Railroad Station, designed by McKim, Mead & White and opened in 1910. The station, with its soaring Doric colonnade and waiting room modeled on the Roman Baths of Caracalla, was destroyed to make way for the less flamboyant Madison Square Garden sports and office complex. What is "Penn Station" today occupies a cramped and dingy corner of its basement. The writer Vincent Scully wryly noted that where formerly "one entered the city like a god...One scuttles in now like a rat."

At least two good things came from that great loss, however. New Yorkers were so outraged that a historic preservation act was finally passed to prevent similar acts of vandalism in the future. And the search was started for a new building to house Penn Station. Senator Patrick Moynihan led the crusade to install the facility in the James A. Farley General Post Office. Not only was it just across Eighth Avenue from the old station and straddling the same tracks below ground, it was coincidentally designed by the same architectural firm of McKim, Mead & White and opened just a few years later, in 1913. It took years to secure permissions and raise funds, but the new Patrick Moynihan Station is scheduled to open in 2004 in the completely renovated interior of this magnificent building, more famous for what it is about to become than what it has been.

The density of buildings that compose Manhattan's famed skyline is so great that sometimes the best way to appreciate it properly is to view it from somewhere else, for example, from Staten Island Roosevelt Island, or here across the Hudson River in New Jersey.

In spite of the fact that it is no longer the tallest of Manhattan's skyscrapers, the slender Empire State Building continues to hold center stage. The colors of its tower lights are changed to honor events, holidays, seasons, and New York's many nationalities. The building glows green on St. Patrick's Day and red on St. Valentine's Day; red and yellow in the fall and red and green for the Christmas holidays; red, yellow, and green on Portugal Day and green, white, and orange for India Independence Day; and of course red, white, and blue for Armed Forces Day, Memorial Day, and the Fourth of July. During spring and fall, when visibility is poor, the lights are turned off to prevent migrating birds from being attracted to the building and crashing into it. The building is darkened on AIDS Awareness Day, which is observed as a "Day without art / Night without lights."

CHELSEA PIERS

The original pink granite buildings of Chelsea Piers opened in 1910 to welcome passengers traveling on the grand ocean liners of the White Star and Cunard lines. Although one ship scheduled to arrive in April of 1912 never made it—the ill-fated *Titanic*—the piers welcomed both the rich and famous and the huge throngs of immigrants of the 1920s and 30s. The Great Depression, however, marked the beginning of the end of transatlantic luxury liner travel, and also a decline of the piers that lasted until the Chelsea Piers Sports and Entertainment Complex opened in 1995. This privately financed, $100-million project transformed the historic piers into a popular center for public recreation.

TWILIGHT

New York might have become a city with no sunlight had zoning laws not been passed to limit the height of new buildings. But what about low constructions, such as churches and theaters, that don't make use of the space above them? Under real estate laws that might sound lunatic anywhere but in New York, the lower buildings can sell "air rights" to developers of adjacent property, who can then build taller structures than they would normally be allowed to. But that air is not cheap. Twenty-five Broadway theaters were recently given the go-ahead to sell rights to the space above their houses to developers in the Theater District. Total price? $100 million.

PLAYING THE BLUES

The origins of jazz lie in the ragtime and blues music brought by African-Americans from the plantations into the inner cities, after the abolition of slavery. Those musical influences followed the northbound routes of African-American migration, up the Mississippi River, from New Orleans to Chicago. Although New York was not as important to the early development of jazz and blues as were those cities, it was nonetheless extremely important in popularizing the new styles. The first jazz recordings were made in New York City, in 1917, as well as perhaps the earliest classic blues recording, *Crazy Blues*, by Mamie Smith in 1920. Here, blues signer Ted Williams performs at a street fair.

140

JAZZ IN NEW YORK

During the Prohibition years, in the early 1920s, New York became the center of jazz in America. Until then, Chicago claimed this title, but strict enforcement of the ban on alcohol in that city put clubs out of business, and jazz musicians out of work. The more loosely policed New York provided a more congenial environment for these musicians. Louis Armstrong was among the many jazz greats who made the move. From the Cotton Club in Harlem to the Roseland Ballroom on 51st Street, jazz fans took their favorite music mainstream in the 1930s. By the 1950s there were so many midtown jazz clubs that 52nd Street was known simply as "Swing Street."

Who would have thought that a neighborhood Irish pub would become the focus of such intense artistic and literary scrutiny? First came John Sloan, an American painter of what was dubbed the "Ashcan School," due to the penchant of its artists for the gritty and realistic portrayal of city scenes. Sloan was so taken with McSorley's that he painted it a number of times between 1912 and 1930. *Life* magazine ran a feature on the increasingly well-known pub and Joseph Mitchell wrote about it in *The New Yorker*, essays that were later featured in his book *McSorley's Wonderful Saloon*.

Today one gets the feeling that McSorley's must look exactly as it did in times past. Browning pictures and memorabilia droop from the walls, sawdust on the floor sops up spilled beer, and the dust on the lighting fixtures appears at least a century old. The character is still there, however, not on a weekend night when tourists line up to get a glimpse of a real New York classic, but on any given weekday afternoon, when the bawdiness and brogue still fill the air.

MCSORLEY'S OLD ALE HOUSE

One of several contenders for the title of oldest pub in the city, this venerable establishment was called the Old House at Home when founded by John McSorley in 1854. The present name was adopted in 1908, two years before John McSorley died at the age of 87. His son Bill ran the establishment until 1936, when he finally sold it. Beer sales didn't take the slightest dip during Prohibition years (1920–33), as politicians made up a sizable portion of the clientele. Old-timers fondly recall that both father and son would personally open the bar each and every day, and buy the last round for their loyal patrons each and every night.

APARTMENT BUILDING, LOWER EAST SIDE

Housing has always been a problem in New York, especially in Manhattan, where limited space has made apartments rather than houses the norm for living quarters. The mid-nineteenth century saw the birth of the tenement, a multiple family dwelling, usually of four stories and built on standard lots 25 feet wide and 100 feet deep. With four apartments to a floor and dark, unventilated interior rooms, as well as the absence of toilet facilities and even running water, most tenements became instant slums. The 1880s saw the first co-ops—buildings owned by their residents. The ground-floor areas of these buildings are typically rented to commercial concerns in order to lower costs to residents.

ANDROMEDA TATTOO PARLOR, EAST VILLAGE

Tattooing as a method of body adornment is as old as the human race. Tools that are thought to have been used for tattooing have been found at several European archaeological sites dating from 10,000 to 40,000 B.C. The Bronze Age man discovered in 1991 frozen in a glacier in the Alps bore several tattoos.

Modern mechanical tattooing was invented in New York City. According to *The Encyclopedia of New York City*, the first mechanical tattoo shop was opened in Chatham Square in 1875 by one Samuel F. O'Reilly, who devised the first electric tattoo machine by modifying the electric engraving pen invented by Thomas Edison.

Credited with popularizing tattooing in the city are O'Reilly's two apprentices, Charlie Wagner, who expanded his mentor's shop into a much larger tattoo-supply business, and Ed Smith, who created hundreds of different tattoo designs. In tattooing lingo, these are called "flash," after carnival slang for something with strong visual attraction.

"SUBWAY SERIES" GRAFFITI

In the city's ethnic neighborhoods, graffiti can be a fine art, a vehicle for expressing hopes and dreams, joys and sorrows. Here on the Lower East Side, street artists have depicted the meeting of two local teams, the Mets and the Yankees, in the World Series held in 2000 in New York. All seven games took place in the city, and this meant that by simply hopping on a number 4 or number 7 train, dedicated baseball fans could see their team play in all the games of this "Subway Series," the first time this has happened in New York in 44 years. Yankees fans were happier than most; their team won the series.

YANKEE STADIUM, THE BRONX

The most well-known baseball stadium in the world is home to the most recognized baseball team in the world, the New York Yankees, and is sometimes called "the house that Ruth built," after the most famous baseball player of all time, Babe Ruth. It was Ruth's popularity that forced the then Yankees owner Jacob Ruppert to leave the Polo Grounds, where the team had been playing, and find a new home just across the Harlem River. The first triple-tiered sports arena ever built, Yankee Stadium opened on April 18, 1923, when the home team beat the Red Sox four to one on a three-run homer by Babe Ruth.

HIGH BRIDGE

One of the most elegant bridges over the Harlem River is High Bridge (seen in the foreground). It was completed in 1842 as part of a masonry aqueduct system to deliver water from the Croton River, 40 miles to the north, to an increasingly populous and thirsty city. Designed to "lend to New York some of the grandeur of imperial Rome," according to its first chief engineer, five of its 80-foot stone arches were unfortunately replaced by a single steel arch in 1937. The bridge, which no longer delivers water, has suffered decades of neglect, but plans are underway to resurrect it as a pedestrian walkway and cycle path between the Bronx and Manhattan.

The Harlem River is in fact an 8-mile tidal channel that connects the East River with the Hudson River (seen in the far distance), and is what really makes Manhattan an island. Since the river separates the 1.5 million people of Manhattan (on the left) from their 1.2 million fellow New Yorkers living in the Bronx (on the right), numerous bridges cross it—ten in all. Although a narrow waterway, the Harlem River is navigable, and its bridges must allow river traffic to pass. The bridge in the foreground rises to allow boats through while the bridges further north turn 90 degrees.

The first bridge across the river was built by wealthy landowner Alexander Macomb, who had built a four-story, tidal-powered gristmill near the river on the Manhattan side, and then purchased a tract of land on the opposite bank, in what was then part of Westchester County. To connect his land to the gristmill, and to provide additional power for it, Macomb proposed a dam and toll bridge, with half of the toll proceeds to go to the poor of New York City. The dam and bridge opened to traffic in 1814, and the new transportation link afforded an economic boost for the area, although the bridge itself was never a moneymaker. But the complex was quite an engineering marvel. The rising tide of the East River would swell through the dam gates, which were then closed; the ebb tide provided power to the gristmill.

BRONX ZOO

The New York Zoological Society (now the Wildlife Conservation Society) was organized in 1895, with the purposes of protecting wildlife and promoting an understanding of zoology through the establishment of a zoological park in New York City. The Bronx Zoo, with 843 animals, was opened to the public in 1899; today the zoo boasts more than 15,000 animals at five New York City facilities. The Congo Gorilla Forest, a 6.5-acre African rainforest habitat, is one of the zoo's many innovative projects. The habitat provides a home to 400 animals of 55 species, including 23 lowland gorillas, one of the largest and most important breeding groups in North America.

UNISPHERE, FLUSHING MEADOW-CORONA PARK

A number of structures in Flushing Meadow-Corona Park remain from the World's Fair held here in 1964–65, the most visible being this twelve-story model of the world constructed by the United States Steel Corporation. Dubbed the Unisphere, it was designed to simulate a view of the earth as it would appear from some 6000 miles in space. The 450-ton structure is formed of an open grid of meridians and parallels, to which are attached curved sheets of stainless steel, with the capitals of the major nations marked in lights. Other nearby holdovers from the last World's Fair include the Singer Bowl, which is now the U.S. Tennis Center.

REFLECTING POOLS, FLUSHING MEADOW-CORONA PARK

The cool reflecting pools and pleasant grounds of Flushing Meadow-Corona Park are relics of the second of three World's Fairs held in New York City. The park, formerly a garbage disposal site known as the Corona Dumps, was leveled and upgraded for the 1939–40 fair. Although a financial failure and beset by problems, the fair was a showcase for technological progress; it was here that the public was introduced to the air-conditioner, the diesel engine, color film, nylon stockings, and television. The second fair held here, in 1964–65, was less remarkable, although it did see the introduction of the Belgian waffle!

SHEA STADIUM

The year 1957 was a gloomy one for New York baseball fans, as both the New York Giants and the Brooklyn Dodgers departed for new homes in California. Attorney and fan William Alfred Shea was instrumental in acquiring a new team for the city. In 1960 the city was awarded one of two new franchises created by the National League, and in 1962 the New York Mets began to play, enticed in part by the promise of a new stadium, which opened in 1964. Capable of switching from a baseball to a football field through the use of motor-operated stands, the stadium was the long-time home of the New York Jets football team as well.

FRIENDS' MEETINGHOUSE, FLUSHING

Quaker missionaries began arriving in the colony that was to become New York City in the mid-seventeenth century. Their belief in pacifism and the "inner light of God" in every individual was regarded with suspicion by the Dutch, and so they tended to settle in outlying areas, including Flushing. Eventually Dutch authorities passed a law forbidding their meetings. One religious dissenter and convert to Quakerism, John Bowne, was arrested and imprisoned for holding meetings in his home. His successful appeal contributed to a growing sense of religious freedom in the new colony. Eventually, in 1694, this meetinghouse, which is still in use, was constructed.

HELL GATE

This ominous name has been given to the narrow channel through which the East River joins the Atlantic Ocean via Long Island Sound. Because of its treacherous tides and rocky shoals, hundreds of wrecked ships lie on the bottom here. These include the *Hussar*, a British frigate that sank in 1780, supposedly carrying a million dollars in gold and silver. In fact, the name Hell Gate derives not from navigational dangers, but from the Dutch name *Hellegat*, which means "beautiful pass." Behind the Triborough Bridge in the foreground can be seen the graceful curve of the Hell Gate Arch, a railroad bridge joining Wards Island with Queens, built in 1917.

STEINWAY PIANO FACTORY, ASTORIA, QUEENS

Steinway & Sons was founded in 1853 by German immigrant Henry Engelhard Steinway, and his sons Henry, Jr., Albert, and Charles. First located in a loft in Lower Manhattan, the company moved to the present 11-acre site in Queens in 1876, where it has since remained. Here, in 400,000 square feet of work space, 600 employees, including immigrants from many nations, make or assemble the up to 12,000 component parts that make up the modern Steinway concert grand piano. Eight different kinds of wood, including maple, mahogany, birch, spruce, poplar, and more exotic species from around the world, are still cut, glued, bent, and shaped mostly by hand. While its competitors produce about 250,000 pianos annually, Steinway finishes only a dozen in a day, the same rate of production as a century ago.

One of the most unusual processes is assembling and bending the rim. Eighteen slats of cured rock maple, each a quarter inch thick, about a foot wide, and up to 23 feet long, are run through a gluing machine, aligned, and bent around a custom-made press. It is a complex operation requiring a team of six, but the continuous curve that results both gives the grand piano its distinctive look and makes a better-sounding instrument.

"A Steinway is a Steinway," said the great pianist Arthur Rubinstein, "and there is nothing else like it in the world." The proof of the piano is in its sound, and Steinway pianos are preferred by a staggering 90 percent of piano soloists performing with major symphony orchestras. Steinway pianos have been played by composers such as Richard Wagner and Franz Liszt, pianists Van Cliburn and Vladimir Horowitz, songwriters George Gershwin and Billy Joel, and jazz stars Harry Connick, Jr., and Keith Jarrett. Most are convinced that only a handmade piano can produce a "sound with a soul." In an age of mass production, Steinway remains a testament to the enduring value of individual craftsmanship.

Steinway pianos are made in a sprawling 27-building plant in Astoria, Queens, which dates back to just after the Civil War, and its outstanding products are still built largely by hand. Most other manufacturers of that era have long since gone out of business or fled the city, but Steinway & Sons endures, a local institution that gave its name to the main street in Astoria, Queens.

The engineering of the Brooklyn Bridge was ahead of its time in several respects and that fact was to prove very costly. The instigator of the project, engineer John A. Roebling was the inventor of spun wire cable. It was this accomplishment that involved him in bridge building, a natural application of the new technology. In 1869, just as construction was to get underway, he was killed in a ferry-boat accident, and his son Washington Roebling took over the project.

There were dangers below and above the bridge. To excavate the riverbed down to the reliable bedrock, workmen labored inside caissons, huge wooden boxes without bottoms that were lowered into the water and fed with compressed air. Working long hours under the high atmospheric pressure and then returning quickly to the surface, many workers were afflicted with caisson disease, today known as the bends. Three men died of the illness and Washington Roebling himself fell victim to it in 1872. He never returned to the bridge, but instead watched the progress through a telescope from his townhouse. Stringing cable between the towers was also dangerous; a flying wire took off one rigger's head and sent another headlong into the river. Another was killed instantly when a cable caught his leg and he was rolled into a drum on which wire was wound. In all, 27 men were killed building the bridge. And, as a final irony, on the day the bridge was opened to the public in 1883, a voice from the crowd warned that the bridge was collapsing. In the ensuing panic, twelve more people died.

HASIDIC CHILDREN AT PLAY, BOROUGH PARK, BROOKLYN

After escaping Portuguese persecution in Brazil and then pirates on the open seas, 23 Jews arrived in New Amsterdam in 1654 aboard the ship *St. Charles*. These first Jews in the new colony were Sephardic, of Spanish and Portuguese descent; Ashkenazi, German Jews, began arriving much later, in the 1830s. Jews thrived in the free economic and political climate of the New World, and soon joined the ranks of the city's leading businessmen, financiers, and intellectuals. These children are Hasidim, members of a religious order devoted to the strict observance of Jewish law.

NEW YORK, NEW YORK

Welcome to the Big Apple! Here we are looking chiefly at Manhattan, whose 23 square miles comprise less than a tenth of the city, but we can see two of the other five boroughs—Brooklyn (in the foreground) and Queens (at the upper right). According to *The Encyclopedia of New York City*, the nickname "Big Apple" was black slang for New York in the 1920s and 30s, and was resurrected in the 1970s as part of a publicity campaign for the New York Convention and Visitors Bureau. Besides the eight million people who live here, nearly 40 million tourists arrive annually. New Yorkers are happy to welcome them, as they will spend more than $17 billion.

WILLIAMSBURG BRIDGE

The longest and heaviest suspension bridge in the world when completed in 1903, the Williamsburg Bridge joins Manhattan with the Williamsburg section of Brooklyn (in the foreground). Williamsburg has exhibited an evolution typical of New York City neighborhoods. Home to wealthy Germans and Irish in the mid-nineteenth century, and poor and working-class Eastern European Jews after the turn of the century, it is now inhabited mainly by Puerto Ricans and Dominicans, who have moved there in the last several decades. Its low rents and old industrial lofts, reminiscent of SoHo, have made it a destination also for artists looking for cheap space. In times past a slum, it is now hip.

JAPANESE GARDEN,
BROOKLYN BOTANIC GARDEN

With the cherry blossoms of spring blazing behind it, the *torii*, or Shinto gate, of this Japanese garden might lead visitors to believe they were in Kyoto rather than Brooklyn. Indeed, this is one of the finest Japanese gardens outside of Japan and the first to be created in a public space in America, opening in 1915 in the Brooklyn Botanic Garden. The Japanese garden is the creation of landscape designer Takeo Shiota, who was born in a small village about 40 miles from Tokyo, and spent his formative years exploring the natural landscape of his native land on foot. In 1907 he came to America, with the avowed goal to create "a garden more beautiful than all others in the world." Through the generous patronage of Botanical Garden trustee Alfred T. White, he was able to realize his dream.

The hill-and-pond style of the Japanese Garden traces its roots back to ancient East Asian designs, and is created to present different views to the stroller at every turn. Taken together, the multitude of perspectives reflects the diversity of nature, especially as perceived by inhabitants of a mountainous island nation with a rocky coastline. To achieve this effect, the garden includes a waterfall, a pond, and an island. Numerous dwarfed trees, carefully placed rocks, and sculpted hills, set against a backdrop of tall forest trees, create the impression of a space far larger than it really is. Stone lanterns and a small Shinto shrine emphasize its Japanese heritage.

CHERRY ESPLANADE, BROOKLYN BOTANIC GARDEN

Unlike other botanical gardens, which were primarily devoted to university research, the focus of the Brooklyn Botanic Garden on the education of the general public was unusual; in 1914 it even established the world's first gardening program for children. The existence of the garden is largely due to the philanthropy of Brooklynite Alfred T. White, who matched funds provided by the city of New York. One of the most popular events on the Brooklyn Botanic Garden's annual calendar is the spring *Sakura Matsuri*, or Cherry Blossom Festival, celebrating the flowering of more than three dozen varieties of Japanese cherry trees along the famous Cherry Esplanade.

BOARDWALK, CONEY ISLAND

At one time Coney Island was the undisputed entertainment center of the world. On an average summer day in 1904, more than 90,000 people would visit Luna Park, only one of several great amusement parks built along the shore. "If Paris is France," wrote George Tilyou, who opened Coney Island's Steeplechase Park in 1897, "then Coney Island, between June and September, is the world." However, many things in New York are not as they once were, and Coney Island, for good or ill, is one. While summer weekend crowds still throng to the 3.5-mile boardwalk with its thrill rides, snack shops, and sandy beaches, on weekdays seagulls seem the majority population.

New York City has always been a working port, and thus not known for its great beaches. In fact, most of the boroughs do have beaches; notable are Orchard Beach in the Bronx, South and Midland Beaches on Staten Island, Rockaway Beach in Queens, and, of course, Coney Island and Brighton Beach in Brooklyn. Even Manhattan, which has not enjoyed a real beach in many years, is planning to reconstruct one along the East River at Turtle Bay.

Still, the city's population makes for crowded and overtaxed beach facilities, so when New Yorkers want to get away they usually head further east, to one of the many fine beaches on the south shore of Long Island. The wealthier or more well-connected you are, the farther you go. The goal is to have a spot all the way out to the end of Long Island, among the mansions and summer homes of the Hamptons. The problem is that on any given summer weekend, the population of the Hamptons swells prodigiously, so that real estate and restaurant prices are today as outrageous as back in Manhattan. And it's not easy to get away from it all when everyone you hoped to leave behind goes with you.

STATEN ISLAND FERRIES

In 1609 Henry Hudson named the island south of Manhattan *Staaten Eyelandt*, after the "States General," the governing body of the Netherlands. Ferry charters from Staten Island to Manhattan date from 1713. Cornelius Vanderbilt, America's great nineteenth-century railroad baron, was born on Staten Island, and started his transportation empire with a regular ferry service as a teenager in 1810. Today the Staten Island Ferry is run by the New York Department of Transportation. Every day 60,000 passengers take the 25-minute, 6-mile boat ride. Free for passengers and bicycles (cars are three dollars), it is acclaimed the best tourist bargain in the world.

BATTERY WEED AND VERRAZANO NARROWS BRIDGE

Fort Wadsworth, nestled beneath the soaring Verrazano Narrows Bridge in a quiet pocket of Staten Island, is the oldest continually manned military reservation in the United States; a fort occupied the site as early as 1663. The reason for the location of both bridge and fort, with its long-silent gun emplacements of Battery Weed shown here, is one and the same: this is the "Narrows," where the boroughs of Staten Island and Brooklyn are closest, and through which enemy ships had to pass to enter New York Harbor (Lower Manhattan can be seen in the distance). Still, when opened in 1964, the 4260-foot main span made it the longest suspension bridge in the world.

HISTORIC HOUSES, RICHMOND TOWN

Aside from many place names, from Brooklyn (after the Dutch village of Breuckelen) to Amsterdam Avenue, there is little physical evidence to remind New Yorkers of their city's founding by the Dutch East India Company. Much of what does exist is here at historic Richmond Town, where 27 original buildings on a 100-acre site represent three centuries of daily life and culture on Staten Island. In season, costumed interpreters and crafts people re-enact daily life in this rural hamlet. Visitors can tour such early structures as Voorlezer's House (top left), built around 1695 by the Dutch Reformed Church as a place of worship and school.

HISTORIC RICHMOND TOWN

The long coastline and protected waters of Staten Island made it very early a center for fishing, oyster harvesting, and boat building. Historic Richmond Town was thought to have been called Cocclestown, after the nearby clams and oysters, when it was founded around 1700. The "old Dutch fisherman" here is neither old nor actually fishing, but is simply a volunteer, Norm Pederson, out to add color to and attract interest in the historical preservation work going on at Richmond Town. In fact, Norm is a skilled "white cooper," who makes household items such as wash buckets and butter churns in the traditional manner in one of Richmond Town's workshops.

VICTORY DINER

Many people wrongly believe that all diners are converted railroad cars; in fact the vast majority are simply prefabricated restaurants designed to capture that "dining car" look. During the 1920s and 30s thousands of diners were built by more than a dozen companies; aficionados can distinguish between manufacturers and models as car buffs can automobiles. Although dictionaries define "diner" as a "restaurant resembling a railroad car," there is no widely accepted agreement on what this entails, says Ron Saari, who manages the authoritative dinercity.com website. A dining-car shape and liberal use of Formica, stainless steel, and glass are typical, as is the inclusion of a counter with stools.

VICTORY DINER—A FAVORITE AMONG LOCALS

A diner is the quintessential neighborhood eatery, a place to meet the locals and have a chat over coffee, which is why presidential candidates—Bob Dole and Bill Clinton, for example—often choose to kick off their campaigns in a classic diner. Built in 1929, the Victory Diner first stood at the corner of Manor Road and Victory Boulevard, near the Halloran General Army Hospital. When its loyal customer base dwindled with the closing of the hospital in 1964, it was moved to its current location. The Pappas family, which has owned the business since the 1940s, heartily endorses the "Ten Commandments of Diners," the first of which is "Thou shall not eat fast food!"

STATEN ISLAND LIGHTHOUSE

The reefs and sand bars of the several channels leading to New York Harbor have always been treacherous; so in 1764, a lighthouse was built at the lower end of New York Bay, off Sandy Hook, New Jersey. It was followed by many others, including the Staten Island Lighthouse, constructed in 1912. This lighthouse was erected specifically to work with the West Bank Lighthouse to aid the navigation of ships seeking to enter the Ambrose Channel, a 10-mile, 45-foot-deep waterway created to provide a safer passage to port facilities.

Staten Island's lighthouse seems incongruously out of place, standing in the midst of a tranquil neighborhood of suburban houses and a golf course, 141 feet above the bay and far from the coastline. Yet due to modern technology, the fixed white light of the unmanned station can be seen for 18 miles down the channel. It is an elegant structure, with an octagonal, sandy-colored brick tower rising 90 feet above a limestone base. It was designated a New York City landmark in 1968 and remains a valuable aid to navigation for all ships entering the Ambrose Channel. It has also become a beloved landmark to Staten Islanders, who now refer to the Richmond Hill neighborhood in which it is located as Lighthouse Hill.

NOON SIESTA, HERALD SQUARE

These two weary gentlemen are snoozing in Herald Square, named after the *New York Herald* newspaper formerly headquartered here. In 1924 it merged with the *New York Tribune* to become the *New York Herald Tribune*. Although that great newspaper, where Tom Wolfe and Jimmy Breslin began their writing careers, ceased publication in 1966, New York City today still supports three major daily newspapers, more than any other American city. The *Tribune* was founded by Horace Greeley, whose statue stands nearby. Greeley is most remembered for his support of western migration, and for widely popularizing the phrase, "Go West, young man."

SELECT BIBLIOGRAPHY

Ashton, Dore. 1972. *New York. World Cultural Guides*. London: Thames and Hudson.

Caro, Robert A. 1974. *The Power Broker: Robert Moses and the Fall of New York*. New York: Alfred A. Knopf.

Dupré, Judith. 1996. *Skyscrapers*. New York: Black Dog & Leventhal.

Edmiston, Susan and Cirino, Linda D. 1991. *Literary New York: A History and Guide*. New York: Peregrine Smith Books.

Everyman Guide to New York. 1994. (Published in North America as the Knopf Guide.) London: David Campbell Publishers.

Eyewitness Travel Guide: New York. 1996. London: Dorling Kindersley.

Geographia New York City Tourist Map. 2000. Weehawken: Geographia Map Company.

Goldberger, Paul. 1979. *The City Observed: New York, A Guide to the Architecture of Manhattan*. New York: Random House.

Jackson, Kenneth T. (ed.). 1995. *The Encyclopedia of New York City*. New Haven and London: Yale University Press.

Kieran, John. 1959. *The Natural History of New York City*. Boston: Houghton Mifflin Company.

Kinkead, Gwen. 1992. *Chinatown: Portrait of a Closed Society*. New York: HarperCollins.

Leeds, Mark. 1991. *Ethnic New York: A Complete Guide to the Many Faces & Cultures of New York*. 1991. Lincolnwood, IL: NTC Publishing Group.

Longstreet, Stephen. 1975. *City on Two Rivers: Profiles of New York—Yesterday and Today*. New York: Hawthorn Books.

Martin, Edwin W. 1868. *The Secrets of the Great City: A Work Descriptive of the Virtues and the Vices, the Mysteries, Miseries and Crimes of New York City*. Philadelphia, PA: Jones, Brothers & Co.

Nash, Eric P. and McGrath, Norman. 1999. *Manhattan Skyscrapers*. New York: Princeton Architectural Press.

Sante, Luc. 1991. *Low Life*. New York: Farrar, Straus & Giroux.

Stern, Robert A. M.; Mellins, Thomas and Fishman, David. 1995. *New York 1960*. New York: The Monacelli Press.

Willensky, Elliot and White, Norval. 1988. *AIA Guide To New York City*. (Third edition.) New York: Harcourt Brace Jovanovich Publishers.

Wilson, Rufus R. 1947. *New York in Literature: The Story Told in the Landmarks of Town and Country*. Elmira, NY: The Primavera Press.

Wright, Carol von Pressentin. 1983. *New York: Blue Guide*. New York: W.W. Norton & Co., Inc.

WEBSITES

www.centralparknyc.org

www.nycparks.completeinet.net

www.nyctourist.com

www.nycvisit.com

www.nyhistory.com

www.nysearch.net

INDEX